LIBERATION THROUGH LAND RIGHTS IN THE PERUVIAN AMAZON

Pedro García Hierro
Søren Hvalkof
Andrew Gray

IWGIA Document No. 90
Copenhagen 1998

LIBERATION THROUGH LAND RIGHTS IN UCAYALI, PERU

Editors: Alejandro Parellada and Søren Hvalkof

Copyright: The authors and IWGIA (International Work Group for Indigenous Affairs)

ISBN: 87-90730-05-4
ISSN: 0105-4503

Traduction from Spanish: Elaine Bolton

Cover, maps and layout: Jorge Monrás

Prepres: Christensen Fotosats & Repro
Copenhagen, Denmark

Print: Eks-Skolens Trykkeri aps
Copenhagen, Denmark

INTERNATIONAL WORK GROUP FOR INDIGENOUS AFFAIRS
Fiolstraede 10, DK 1171 - Copenhagen K, Denmark
Tel: (+45) 33 12 47 24 - Fax: (+45) 33 14 77 49
E-mail: iwgia@iwgia.org

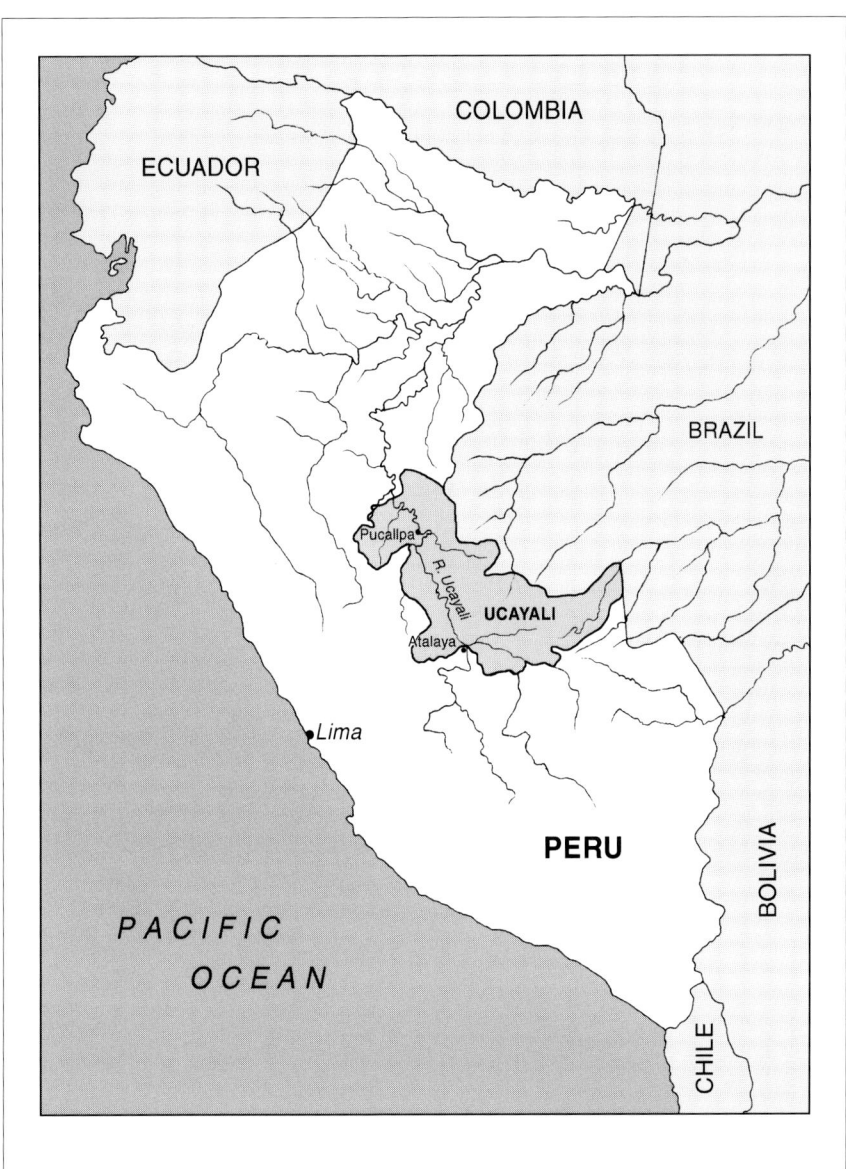

CONTENTS

Foreword: 9

Atalaya: Caught in a Time Warp

by Pedro García Hierro 15

**From Slavery to Democray:
The Indigenous Process of Upper
Ucayali and Gran Pajonal**

by Søren Hvalkof 83

**Demarcating Development:
Titling Indigenous Territories in Peru**

by Andrew Gray 165

Photographers 219

FOREWORD

Ucayali is one of the provinces of the Peruvian Amazon whose economy is based on the extraction of natural resources. From the time of the boom in the rubber economy until the beginning of this century the region supplied the national and international markets with rubber. Covering an area of more than one hundred thousand sq. km., its indigenous population belong to the Asháninka, Ashéninka, Yine, Shipibo, Amahuaca, Yaminahua, Cashinahua and Sharanahua groups.

Indigenous peoples, in Ucayali as in other parts of the world, consider the demarcation and titling of their territories to be one of their principal demands. In the case of Ucayali, this demand was an urgent need given the serious human rights violations that were being committed against the indigenous population.

Ever since the presence of Europeans in this Amazonian region, the extraction of natural resources in Ucayali has only been possible through subjection of the indigenous people to a system of slave labour. In January 1986, complaints were for the first time presented by indigenous Asháninka to the national indigenous organisation, AIDESEP, denouncing the mistreatment inflicted on them by the patrons of Atalaya. AIDESEP thus began organising a series of visits to the zone in order to document hundreds of similar cases. The system known as "enganche" or "habilitación" was general practised, in which a debt towards a patron was repaid with work. In this way, a pair of trousers or a machete could be the equivalent of one year's labour. To this abuse could be added the kidnapping of children, the rape of women, the incarceration of indigenous people and harsh punishment of all attempts at protest or escape. And all of these atrocities were carried out with the approval of the local authorities.

The presence of AIDESEP in the zone initially encouraged the escape of some captives, an increase in protests and fear on the part of the authorities. Months later visits to the zone by two commissions, one from the International Labour Organisation and one from the Peruvian Indigenous Institute, were carried out. The official conclusions confirmed serious human rights abuses. In order to regularize the situation the urgent recognition and titling of native communities was recommended.

Meanwhile, the situation in Atalaya was getting even worse. The communities were now also caught in the crossfire between anti-indigenous guerrilla movements, the counter-insurgency forces of the State and the drug-traffickers.

At the same time, the indigenous organisational process was rapidly gaining strength. In September 1987, the Asháninka established the Regional Indigenous Organisation of Atalaya, OIRA, and together with AIDESEP they formulated a strategy to recover their lands and put an end to the abuse. A similar process had been taking place in the neighbouring district of Gran Pajonal where the Ashéninka organisation, OAGP, had titled some of their communities.

Following intense negotiations, AIDESEP subsequently signed an Agreement with the Ministry of Agriculture for the demarcation and titling of the communities. Given the Peruvian State's lack of financial resources, IWGIA was thus presented with an ambitious programme of territorial planning in Ucayali, taking the zone of Atalaya as its starting point.

In order to obtain the necessary funding, IWGIA approached the Danish government through its international cooperation agency, DANIDA. The response was positive and in 1989 a programme began which was implemented in three phases, ending in 1998. During this period difficult work was carried out with impressive results: the territorial legalisation of more than 200 indigenous communities was achieved, recognition of three reserves for peoples in voluntary isolation was gained and studies for four communal reserves were drawn up. The project also meant the withdrawal of a significant number of the patrons responsible for the mistreatment of the indigenous population.

At the same time, thousands of indigenous people who did not exist in official statistics were registered, enabling their participation in local elections and achieving, for the first time, access to municipalities such as Atalaya by the indigenous leaders.

The project was innovative in several ways. Firstly, it took as its starting point the definition of communal boundaries by the indigenous themselves, according to their needs, attempting to demarcate the communities in such a way that they bordered on to each other and thus created continuous territories.

Secondly, the project was implemented wholly by the indigenous organisation and its technical team, with no permanent presence in Peru on the part of IWGIA staff. In our opinion, this system of cooperation has enabled the indigenous organisation to gain strong experience in the overall management of large-scale projects, both in the planning of activities and in administrative procedures. The organisation also made excellent achievements in the difficult negotiation process with the authorities. Lastly, costs have been amongst the lowest in Peru for a titling project.

The project was also a great challenge for IWGIA. Our organisation, whose main activity is the documentation and dissemination of information regarding the situation of indigenous peoples,
did not have sufficient experience in handling projects of this size. We were learning, along with AIDESEP, through the countless problems which arise in a programme of this kind. We chose to supervise the project through periodic brief visits to Peru and to incorporate the project within IWGIA's general programme of activities, which covers the exchange of experiences with other indigenous peoples, research work and participation in international processes such as those of the United Nations.

This book is an attempt to reflect on the process which made this project possible. In the first section the lawyer, Pedro García Hierro, who was advisor to AIDESEP and to the titling project, gathers together some of the testimonies from enslaved indigenous people which served as the basis for support of the project, together with a socio-legal analysis of the situation.

In the second article the anthropologist, Søren Hvalkof, covers the history of the Atalaya and Gran Pajonal region based on his personal experience. Lastly the anthropologist, Andrew Gray, describes and analyses the actual implementation of the project.

The Ucayali titling project has been more than just a process of legalisation of indigenous lands. It has also represented a valuable contribution to the process of democratisation in the zone. In this way, the indigenous peoples are now demanding a fairer relationship with national society.

The titling of indigenous territories is not an end in itself, but one step in the process towards self-management. We thus consider it essential that this process be continued and that external cooperation continues to support indigenous peoples' participation in local and national political power and in the creation of an indigenous economy.

Jens Dahl
IWGIA Director

Alejandro Parellada
Projects Coordinator

ATALAYA, CAUGHT IN A TIME WARP

Pedro García Hierro

The importance of the contribution of each one of the indigenous peoples of the world to the improvement of living conditions in the "global village" has been greatly debated throughout this final decade of the century. Nevertheless, whilst the political arena opens up ever more economic spaces, freeing-up all kinds of investment from legal, work-related, ecological or ethical obstacles, it is rare for an indigenous peoples to be provided with the incentive or minimum conditions to put their wisdom into practice and demonstrate their capacity to move towards the future from an alternative perspective.

A couple of years ago, the Asháninka people of the Central Rainforest of Peru caused a stir, bringing to light a very commercially successful natural medicine: "uña de gato", one of the remedies which has aroused the greatest interest amongst researchers into illnesses such as AIDS and cancer. Any Asháninka woman over 35 could talk for hours about hundreds of other resources and therapeutic procedures of a similar value. While, as in the case of the Huitotos of Putumayo - whose misfortune it was to discover the use of rubber, a product which revolutionized world trade and transport and drove them to the point of extinction - the Asháninkas have experienced an avalanche of new invasions onto their territories and a reduction in their living area from "uña de gato".

And if this is the response to their creativity, what are their daily living conditions? The circumstances of the Asháninka people over the past one hundred years have been particularly violent.

The miserable privilege of having their territories opened up to road networks and other market benefits since the end of the last century displaced the Asháninka from the Chanchamayo, Paucartambo, Chorobamba and Huancabamba valleys. The invasion was massive. 'Those who did not die in the clashes with settlers or did not move to, as yet, uncolonized areas became confined to ever smaller areas of land' (Santos and Barclay,1995). Nevertheless, by buying back their own ancestral lands from a foreign company - the Peruvian Corporation Ltd., to whom the Peruvian government had granted two million hectares of Asháninka territory in 1891 - they had begun to reorganize their lives by the middle of the 20th century, adapting to the new conditions, so different from those which had supported their reproduction throughout the centuries.

With the small plots of land which they recovered, they managed to reestablish themselves and develop coffee growing businesses, new communities and an incipient modern political organization.

However, very soon the disorganized incursion of new settlers and the subsequent frustration of their hopes turned the Central Rainforest into a veritable hell. By 1984 the Apurímac, Ene and Puerto Ocopa valleys were invaded by coca growers spurred on by the drugs dealers and then, immediately after, Sendero Luminoso (Shining Path) began its brutal appearance in the region. The MRTA (Revolutionary Movement Tupac Amaru) gathered force and were installed in the Pichis and Palcazú valleys.

In December 1989, the murder of the pinkatzari, Alejandro Calderón, at the hands of the MRTA, dragged the Asháninka people into a war whose roots were planted deep in the very policy of colonization of their ancestral territories. For six long years the Asháninka people were leading characters in one of the stormiest chapters of Peruvian history.

Whilst in Lima people experienced the news and frights of the terror, the Asháninka people, more than any other civilian population, organized their forces within the forest and fought, for the benefit of the whole population of Peru, in defence of the dignity, rights and lands which Peru had denied them for more than a century. It was, at least initially, an initiative which inconvenienced the regular army considerably, as it had been incapable of achieving in five years what the ovayeriite - the autonomous Asháninka army - achieved within a short time of their establishment. They rescued thousands of captive Asháninkas and recovered wide tracts of territory occupied by the armed groups.

This sacrifice signified a first step towards the pacification of the country and served as an example to other peoples to face up to their liberation.

The 'war report' which the Asháninka organizations delivered to the country in 1996 is devastating:

'In order to achieve (peace) the Asháninka people has seen more than 3,500 of its sons and daughters, men, women and children, cruelly die. The population of more than 50 communities was obliged to abandon their homes and become displaced. More than 5,000 Asháninkas were taken captive and some still remain prisoners today. More than 10,000 Asháninkas have been forcibly displaced and left with no home and no means of survival. For 6 years we have all lived on a war footing and have been the targets of harassment, assassinations, night raids, torture and massacre of a large number of our leaders.

And today you live in peace.

The genocide and the suffering of the Asháninka family is of tragic proportion and has seriously compromised our existence as a people in a number of ways:

- Emotionally:

The trauma of having witnessed acts of brutality such as the loss of families and communities through murder, the cruel treatment of prisoners at the hands of Sendero, slavery and forced labour, the destruction of houses, schools, centres and entire communities, continual displacement from one area to another.

- Socially:

The breakdown of family life; isolation and abandonment; many women are now widows and many children now orphans; many young people have disappeared or died.

- Culturally:

Limitations on the practice of our traditional way of life; loss of knowledge, as many elderly people have faced violent and premature death; clashes with a new and hostile cultural reality; encounters with negative and aggressive social elements such as the drug traffickers and Sendero.

- Economically:

Paralysis in production due to the need for self-defence; in the case of the refugees and displaced, the loss of all belongings, equipment and tools along with their lands, total lack of food and economic income with the consequent proliferation of illnesses and malnutrition.

We do not deserve this state of affairs, which we have suffered in order to gain peace for you. To consolidate peace in Peru, the Asháninka people must have the right to live', (Statement to the Nation signed by the Asháninka Emergency Committee, 1996).

But whilst the government has achieved recognition and incomparable electoral support through peace being achieved, the Asháninka people, who contributed to this peace, are living through a new chapter of outrage. The return to their lands is being frustrated and it is the government itself which is encouraging a new invasion of the communal lands to the benefit of, amongst others, reformed ex-Senderistas.

Forestry contracts awarded to large timber companies in the Pangoa - during the very period of maximum violence - prevent recognition of the territorial rights of the displaced Asháninka, condemning them to hopeless exile. Oil companies have set up on Asháninka land, inevitably attracting migrants.

These are the circumstances in which indigenous peoples such as the Asháninka have to compete with other economic players in order to demonstrate the comparative advantage of their technologies and their knowledge of the sustainable use of resources. Scenes such as these constitute the' universities' in which young indigenous people are trained to face up to the future.

The story which we are now going to present is just one more chapter in the modern history of the Asháninka people and demonstrates the kind of opportunities which national society offers to them for their development.

Atalaya is a small town situated at the point where the rivers Urubamba and Tambo converge to form the Ucayali. It is the only urban centre of any consequence in a large area of the Central Rainforest in which a drop in the international price of rubber and isolation with respect to markets have left the former paymasters spread out over small estates with their 'Indians' and their medieval rights over the family and property of indigenous labourers. Within the sole knowledge of alternatives, slavery came to be considered a natural institution, to such an extent that concerns of an ethical nature never occurred to the "Christian" employers of Atalaya.

The history of the events in Atalaya reveal the nature of the basis of many modern timber companies throughout the Amazonian region.

The fine woods used or exported, the furniture and parquet floors in the shop windows of the shopping centers have had a long journey, a journey which begins in such places as Atalaya, where a large part of the wood produced in Ucayali comes from (Ucayali provides 42% of the sawnwood in Peru and 32% of the laminated and plywood[1].

During the preparatory meetings of the 3rd Intergovernmental Panel on Forests, we had the opportunity of listening to the big industrialists of the Forestry Association and to senior civil servants working in the sector. They were discussing concepts such as indicators of sustainability, technological models to adapt the timber industry to Peru's commitments with the International Tropical Timber Organization, certification of forest management, modernization of the legal and institutional frameworks, productive excellence and total quality, systems of access, externalities, financial frameworks and appropriate tax systems... Having lived through events in Atalaya and noted the modus operandi of the last links in the Amazonian forest chain, all of this progressive paraphernalia seemed a contradiction in terms to us.

It is not fair to consider that those attending the Panel were acting cynically or dishonestly. Situations such as that in Atalaya can only make sense if the other extreme of the production process is unaware of them, if the big industrialists look upwards, towards excellence, towards the global quality market, delegating executive functions to subordinates who, they assume, know how to do their job. When all is said and done, delegation is the modern basis of efficient management.

The story of the events in Atalaya is the horrific discovery of the mass of the iceberg of the free market economy, the part which does not appear in macro-economic figures. It is the price that modernity imposes on those who do not share in its benefits and over whom a veil is thrown, making them invisible so that their suffering does not tarnish the glory of development.

And it is also an odyssey which recounts the strength of a people to recover from the most severe conditions, mobilized by the desire to continue existing.

The suffering of slaves

On 5th January 1986, a humble-looking Asháninka elder visited the offices of the national organization for Peruvian Amazonian indigenous peoples, AIDESEP[2], saying that he had escaped being beaten to death by timber company employers whilst trying to defend the last ten hectares of land on which he and all his relatives struggled to survive. On both eyes and on other parts of his body, he bore the clear marks of the cruelty of this aggression.

Mr. Marinero, from Tahuanti, in the headwaters of the Ucayali, told us incredible stories of a land until then unknown to any leader of the modern Peruvian indigenous movement. The Atalaya region was known only as the accursed region where the Sepa Penal Colony, an open prison, had been built, a place whose name inspired terror. ('You don't get out of there alive'). Little else was known of these forgotten and lawless lands.

The then Secretary for Defence and Territory of AIDESEP, the Asháninka Mr. Miqueas Mishari, organized an initial visit to the zone. He arrived unannounced, wearing a cushma[3], on the advice of Mr. Marinero himself. And not without reason. The visit of "an important person" from Lima, coming to check on accusations made by indigenous people was received with such hostility that, from the day of this first visit, Mr. Mishari's head has had a price on it amongst the small landed paymasters of the large timber companies.

The reports of this first visit were so surprising that emergency work was immediately begun, giving priority to making an inventory of, and putting a stop to, the serious human rights violations which the Asháninka, Yíne, Yaminahua and other indigenous peoples of the region were being subjected to.

AIDESEP began by organizing short visits of one week to the region. Slowly, as people overcame their fear of reprisals, accusations began to be made. For the legal staff of AIDESEP, the situation was overwhelming. The indigenous peoples was being subjected to atrocities that were known only in the history books. Atalaya, in the twentieth century, was a contemptible region where racist perversion was considered to be the normal consequence of a natural inferiority. The police, magistrates, and local government employees of the Ministry of Agriculture, 'the authorities', were working to facilitate the inhuman exploitation of the indigenous population by the bosses and paymasters, with the clear certainty that this was right in the eyes of local development.

Some of the complaints described situations which would be identified as a formidable form of slavery, right in the middle of the 20th century. The following transcripts are part of a collection of testimonies prepared by AIDESEP[4].

***

Miqueas Mishari Mofat
AIDESEP Defence Secretary
(The Inter-Ethnic Association for Development of the Peruvian Rainforest)
San Eugenio Avenue no. 981, Santa Catalina,
Lima.

I, Cristobal Ahuarari Campa, 60 years of age and living in the native community of Toniromashi, falling within the Bolognesi district of the Province of Atalaya, Ucayali Department, respectfully present myself before you and state:

That I am father of my children, Rogelio Ahuarari aged 17 and Samuel Ahuarari, Estelita Ahuarari, who are workers on the 'Boca Apinihua' estate belonging to Victor Merino Sharff. Since 1982, they have lived there as slaves, with no payment for their work. In December 1987, my son Rogelio came to the community of Toniromashi in order to free himself from his employer, together with his wife Florinda. After they had been in the community for three days, Victor Merino Sharff turned up, accompanied by 2 civil guards, and tricked them into going back to the estate to continue exploiting them with police support. They said they would return within a month, but they have still not come back, and as their father I am worried for them.

I also want to denounce the act of rape by Mr. Victor Merino Sharff, who raped my daughter-in-law Florinda, wife of Rogelio, on various occasions, threatening her that if she did not accept he would give her nothing to eat. He keeps them working all day and he treats all the female workers of the estate the same, with no respect for their hus-

Children kidnapped by Shining Path and liberated by the Asháninka army

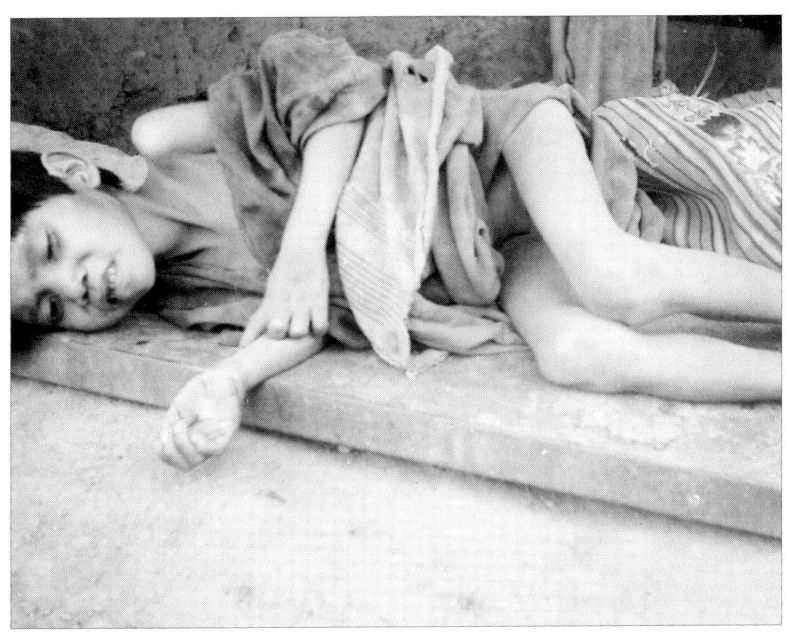

bands. If any one of them dares to complain he threatens them with a gun. This was why Rogelio left, because he could not continue to watch his wife suffer the abuses of the aforementioned hacienda owner, Victor Merino Sharff.

My son has worked as a labourer since 1982 and to this day he has never been paid for his work; he is still in debt because he does not know how to work out his accounts.

***

I, Carlos Tamani Vargas, 54 years of age and resident in the area of Diobamba with ID. No. 00152909, do respectfully present myself before you and state:

That I accuse the estate owner, César Cagna Figueroa, of not having paid me for my 30 years of work on his estate "Chanchamayo", where I spent all my youth working; to this day I have received no kind of settlement or payment, except that last year my mother-in-law was taken ill and he promised to take her to the town of Pucallpa for treatment. On her return he charged me for this. As I do not have any money I am thus burdened with a further debt of 4,000 Intis which, with interest on my mother-in-law's tickets (an ex-worker on the same estate), has now become 11,000 Intis. During the 30 years of my service I have worked every day from 7 in the morning until 6 at night with no lunch, and this is customary. It is the same for all the Asháninka brothers and sisters who have worked for him for many years with no payment. Nevertheless, they are still in his debt, as is my case; this is how he becomes wealthy - through our labour. Most of us are mistreated or beaten with the barrel of a shotgun until we become ill, even the boss's wife treats us like this.

***

I, Gregorio Ríos Panduro, an Asháninka of 30 years of age, with ID. No. 0015900, a resident of the Diobamba native community in Raymondi district, Atalaya province, Ucayali department, have come to your office to make the following complaint to you:

The estate owners, César Cagna Figueroa and his son Capi Cagna, owners of the 'Chanchamayo' estate located in the abovementioned district and province, have illegally appropriated an engine of mine (20 horsepower Peque-Peque), threatening me with physical violence if I showed any resistance. This motor was given to me for work carried out over a number of years and for various employers, but they took it from me claiming that it had been lost and forcing me to work for them again, by removing 200 (two hundred) pieces of timber but I have still been paid nothing and they have not given me my engine back. Thus I have worked for 10 (ten) years with no payment or other settlement.

But I am not the only one to have suffered this wrongdoing, the same thing has happened to 60 Asháninka who have been enslaved on the 'Chanchamayo' estate for many years (between 15 and 30). I now find myself in a situation of anxiety since Mr. Capi Cagna has threatened me with violence because of the complaints I made to the Atalaya Sub-Prefecture and he usually threatens all my compatriots with a gun.

This man has committed a number of assaults on indigenous people, with the aid of two local guards appointed by the estate owner, Hernán Cagna Figueroa. The names of these guards are Daniel Armas and Sebastián Armas, whose responsibility it is to capture anyone who runs away, beat them up and put them in cells built by the indigenous people themselves on the orders of the estate owner.

Because of all of this, I am asking you to intervene in the matter so that this situation of slavery and constant abuse may be brought to an end, not only for me but for all my indigenous brothers who work on the estates of the Cagnas.

This is all I have to say, and I take my leave of you.

***

I am Mrs Amalia Pezo. My husband was working for the timber company of Mr Adan Caña. My husband was healthy but he died whilst working for the mentioned patron.

Thus they give us nothing to eat.

My husband was given only a pot, a plate and a spoon, nothing else.

***

Warm greetings to you, your family and those employed within AIDESEP.

The native community of Diobamba, on the left bank of the river Ucayali, Raymondi district, Atalaya province, wish to denounce the actions of César Cagna Figueroa. We have agreed to complain about the abuse and outrages we have suffered for many years at his hands. He has taken our land away from us in two places: firstly the 'Chanchamayo' estate. He does not work here, he just lives to exploit and deceive us in our work. He has appointed himself Chief of the native community and we are compelled into forced labour. He does not let us talk or laugh. If we stop working or speak, he threatens to hit and beat us. He often kicks and punches us. Most recently, he punched Teobaldo Camaiteri whilst we were moving logs. Already tired with hunger, he could work no longer, which is what we are forced to do. We start work at 6 in the morning and often do not stop until 6.30 in the evening. And he still treats us badly. In another incident he almost killed a young deaf and dumb boy from Unini, hitting him with the barrel of his gun until he escaped, if not he had been killed. We still know nothing about this young person, whether he is dead or alive. Husbands and wives are sent to the forest and the women are never paid. From the moment they go out to when they return. He gives them 4 metres of cloth for their cushmas. That is their payment, whilst their children die of hunger and illness.

The same thing happens on the Pacaya estate. The same César Cagna Figueroa who makes us all work without pay and threatens us, has put himself in charge of the native community. 'If you don't work I will go to Bolognesi and get the police, the governor or the judge to send you all to prison.' To make us afraid he brought the police and took myself, Elías Estalin Quinticuare Nicolás and Elías Sánchez Velásquez, prisoner. He carted us off to the Bolognesi Civil Guard station. And we were kept prisoner for two days in the cells. The Civil Guard and César Cagna got drunk together in his house. We were left with no food or water for two days and they made fun of us. Then they let us go and we were forced to return to work for the same exploitative owner. This abuse has been going on since 1983. Currently, ten men and ten women from my community, which is the place known as 'Tahuania', are working in the timber industry. Even the schoolchildren do not escape. They are also made to work. Last year a pupil known as Santiago Carlos Tamani was sent to work and he never came back. This time it was another pupil from my native community, his younger brother, Leyne Carlos Tamani, 15 years old. We cannot put up with all these abuses any longer. We have no means of complaint. There is no justice for us. They tell us we are just Indians and if they kill us, so what. Through fear of this we have never been able to complain.

Thanks to my compatriot from Chicosa, Manuel Bardales García, who attended the Atalaya conference when you first visited us, we now know that there is somebody willing to help us, and that is AIDESEP. This is why we have come to you today.

We ask you to come and investigate all of the outrages and abuses which have occurred in our community. We also ask for our community to be titled. We are 25 families, 150 adults and children in total. And we ask that you get rid of the exploitative Mr. César Cagna Figueroa. Attached is a sketch of our Community, I have indicated in red where the community was in 1983. We have lived here centuries, since I don't know when. This man has us hidden away so that nobody notices or visits us. Outsiders are forbidden to come here. We can't get in touch with anybody. As you can see on the map, he is on the banks of the river Ucayali and we are behind him; he does not permit us to leave.

We get the barrel of a gun in return for our work, he takes everything away from us, we are allowed nothing. What he takes, he gives to someone else, before taking it away again. This is abuse. We have given up all hope of justice. And we hope our complaint reaches the government and ministers.

***

AIDESEP staff set up a temporary office in an Asháninka house on the outskirts of the town of Atalaya where, come nightfall, the families of victims cautiously came to see us. All they wanted to do was express their grief. They did not believe for one minute that their situation could change after one hundred years of outrage.

In the AIDESEP files, and on the desks of the 'authorities', heart-rending reports were beginning to accumulate.

Children were taken by force from the age of five. The local courts said this was good for them, because their 'godparents' were Christians and their parents only Indian. Entire families and communities bearing the same name (Marinero was the name of more than 50 people in Tahuanti), were assigned to different estate owners. They were kept locked up in barracks under guard and used for the location, cutting and transportation of wood. Payment did not exist, and nor did the most minimal humanitarian considerations. Women were raped in the forest in front of their husbands, and the husband would even be hit with 'metal'[5] if they dared to protest. They worked from sunrise to sunset, come rain or shine and, occasionally, were given paltry amounts of manioc to feed the whole family. Some people report living such a life for more than 30 years.

The AIDESEP staff, and other related volunteers, watched with astonishment the nocturnal appearance of a veritable 'Court of Wonders': crippled children, fathers of sons put down like horses in the forest after a work accident, mothers with their heads cropped for having tried to get their daughters back, labourers with their faces scarred by fire for having wanted to escape the owners' estates, young people blinded for life by machete blows[6].

In Lima nobody could believe the reports and the legal accusations got no further than Pucallpa, if indeed they actually got any further than the local police office.

Nevertheless, the persistence of the accusations began to disturb Atalaya life. Mass escapes began to take place and on every visit the management and staff of AIDESEP had to be protected by dozens of indigenous people when walking through the centre of town. The authorities initially denounced those making the accusations as subversives (Shining Path was at this time becoming a reality in the region), and ignored the numerous assaults on AIDESEP staff by the paymasters.

In 1987, some young girls began to escape from the estate owners' houses. The pictures they painted were heartbreaking. There is a photograph in AIDESEP's files which expresses the crude reality of these night-time sessions which continued for nearly two and a half years. An AIDESEP staff member is typing out accusations on an old typewriter by the light of a candle which is lighting up the image of a young seven year old girl, beaten up by her boss once the judge's decision to free her and return her to her parents became known.

The fact is that custom had created a local law which attributed rights over those who were not considered people at all. Let us give some examples to demonstrate what we mean.

On visiting for the first time the Atalaya Justice of the Peace - himself a descendant of an Asháninka woman and a mestizo estate owner - to claim the freedom of the aforementioned girl, AIDESEP's lawyer and Mr Miqueas Mishari were surprised to hear the words, 'What do you think you are doing? This child has already been baptized by the lady of the house, it belongs to her now'. When legal arguments were put forward, the JP insisted, 'But gentlemen, the mother of this child is an Indian, they know nothing about rights'. Her freedom was at last gained by mentioning the possibility of a complaint of kidnapping being made against the estate owner and this very JP.

On another occasion, a young man came to us at night to denounce torture at the hands of the police. He had the clear marks of cigarettes having been stubbed out on his face. We went to the police station the following morning, where they justified the violence with the following words, 'This guy is very smart. He belongs to Mrs. Edelisa and he has escaped. He owes money and doesn't want to work. You have to show a firm hand because if not, they'd all run away, swindling their bosses.'

In this context, the initial actions were - obviously - very difficult but the incipient doubts of the authorities concerning the regularity of local customs was beginning to give results. The Asháninka population and other regional indigenous peoples were gaining strength through these small victories and beginning to stand up for themselves, to the consequent embarrassment of the authorities and estate owners.

In the middle of 1986 AIDESEP, in an attempt to move the complaints on from the stagnation of the local environment, alleged 'violations of labour laws' before the Indigenous Institute of the Ministry of

Labour. Seventeen estates were subjected to investigations by inspectors not linked to the local situation. They were only allowed entry to four of them, receiving threats from the remainder. But it was enough. Their report was used as an official document to inform the International Labour Organization (ILO) of what was happening in Atalaya.

A commission from the Peruvian Indigenous Institute (IIP) itself, at the request of the ILO, checked the cases in the communities of Tahuanti and Sabaluyo, those closest to Atalaya, in November 1986. Contrary to the declaration of the local office that there were no 'true' indigenous people in the region, even less so in the 'so-called' communities of Tahuanti and Sabaluyo, which 'were settlers' lands', the IIP's eye witness report photographically documented more than 80 people in each place. Apart from giving detailed information on the dispossession of the lands (which had been supported and prompted by local government employees such as Duilio Lucioni, Head of the Agrarian Office) it led to the possibility of the existence of the practice of slavery being considered.

Some extracts and a summary of their conclusions follow:

To reach the aforementioned localities, the author had to travel 18 hours overland from Lima to Satipo, then by light aircraft to Atalaya and a last leg by boat and mountain trail. Perhaps these difficulties of access may explain why the public authorities have not been able to look into the serious situation which the said native populations are going through.

Nevertheless, this report must be followed up with the implementation of new actions, in order to urgently resolve the situation, since it could give rise to serious accusations against the Peruvian State which is in contradiction with ILO Agreement 107, ratified by Peru and enforceable by law since 02.06.68.

Two rivers run through Tahuanti, the Tahuanti and the Contaniva, and the tributary of this, the Camonguyo; all flow into the Chicosillo, which in turn is a tributary of the Ucayali. The existing population of Tahuanti, as recorded in the 'Book of Records of the Native Community', amounts to 88 native Asháninkas, divided into approximately 22 families.

A brief analysis of this population gives us the following table of groups by family name, which are indicative of family ties:

Family groups in Tahuanti.

1. Marinero-Campos family: 15 people
2. Marinero-Chumpate family: 8 people
3. Marinero-Camaiteri family: 10 people
4. Marinero-Lorita family: 14 people

5. Marinero-Sánchez family: 3 people
6. Marinero-Marinero family: 2 people
7. Marinero-Pachacutec family: 3 people
8. Marinero-Napoleon family: 5 people
9. Ríos-Campos family: 3 people
10. Sánchez-Sánchez family: 4 people
11. Others: 13 people
12. People coming into the community: 4 people.

A significant number of these people were registered by photo, the rest were absent looking for means of survival; working for the timber companies, for other settlers or simply moving around the interior due to the strong pressures exercised by the settlers over their lands.

In the opinion of the author, these native populations must have been settled in these areas for at least 50 years or more. This is based on the following information:

-The presence of the elders Ricardo Marinero Campos (Tahuanti) and Moisés Napo Ríos (Sabaluyo), 77 and 75 years of age respectively, who testify that they buried their parents on these very lands which had been theirs since birth.

-The existence of fruit trees (star apple, mango, avocado, coconut) 20, 25, even 30 years old which were noted in the communal areas and photographed on the small farms from which Mr. Ricardo Marinero and his family were evicted.

-The testimony of the very people who question the current existence of the community, as is the case of Mr Duilio Lucioni, who has worked for 13 years in the Agrarian Office of Atalaya and is currently in charge, who stated, 'The Marineros and Napos previously lived along the river Unini as workers of the Michelena brothers. Their mother closed the school which existed in this place, handed the lands over to her son-in-law and moved, together with the native labourers - who previously were her private property - to Santa Rosa which is near to Chicosillo where 8 to 10 native families of the Marinero and Napo settled between 1945 and 1952. The migrants from the mountains began to arrive about four years ago.'

- In trips made to both communities it was possible to observe fallow lands located in the interior and on the extreme boundaries of the territories claimed by both populations, with a distinct level of development and age, between 10 and 15 years, which proves an original native presence in these territories.

The presence of settlers is much more recent, the first immigrants arrived to this area around 1978/79, as can be seen from a review of the certificates of possession granted by the Agrarian Office of Atalaya (OAA).

Up until now, the native population had not been registered individually, let alone as a native community by the offices in Sinamos, the Development Committee of Coronel Portillo or the Ministry of Agriculture which operates in Ucayali.

The natives point out that they feared detention, torture and threats and they had decided to accept the situation and 'loan' their land, including a number of areas under cultivation.

They moved to the Contaniva river, where they found their former fallow lands of these areas occupied by Exímedes Pezo Panduro, who claimed to be the owner through a certificate of possession negotiated without the indigenous people's knowledge.

Faced with this situation of destitution, several of the families went to the interior to look for food, some to the timber companies and the group, along with the head of the native community, decided to return to their lands on the Tahuanti river and take back the motor that was borrowed. Here they came up against an even more serious situation; the large house of the Marineros was burned down, although the wooden posts could still be seen and were photographed and settler B. told them that he was now the owner, with a certificate from the OAA.

A further 20 settlers had invaded their small farms and fallow lands which had been laid to rest. On top of this, illegal trafficking in the buying and selling of their lands had been occurring and everyone said they had the support of the OAA. The invasion now covered the whole native community between the rivers Tahuanti, Camonguylo, Contaniva and Lagarto.

It seems that this illegal trafficking in land was something normal and virtually public. There is no other way of understanding, for example, the existence in the very town of Atalaya of a restaurant two blocks from the OAA and three blocks from the Sub-Prefecture, where there is a large poster advertising the sale of the 100 hectare Chicosillo farm and plantation (this relates to native lands under cultivation that are sold by anyone who can get their hands on them).

The informants refer to the fact that on returning once more without land or food, the natives were forced to locate to an area further from the river Chicosillo in the upper part of Camonguyo and under the 'protection' of the landowner, Mr Pezo.

To get to this place we had to walk one hour across small farms, swamps and woodland. We found native families living on top of each other, in houses they had built themselves. The farms being cultivated were too small to feed the group and they told us that it was prohibited to fish in large quantities and even worse if this was done outside of the area in which they lived. The geographic and human neglect was thus extensive.

Similarly, according to testimonies collected, exploitative, deceitful and coercive working relations were being developed towards the indigenous population on the part of the settlers. The following are some examples of exploitative and unpaid working relations.

Faced with these conflicts, action on the part of the authorities was virtually nil, according to the natives. For example, according to Rogelio Campos Aguilar, in September 1985 he requested the allocation of an area near the Sabaluyo stream and Mr Víctor Sánchez (head of the Rural Settlement of the OAA) replied that, 'you don't have the law on your side, I'll give you a scrap of land but if you want anything larger you'll have to pay one or two million'.

Amongst the settlers, there is a group belonging to the so-called Church of the New Universal Israelite Pact. They are led by Zemiliano Martínez in Tahuanti and Juan Barbarán in Atalaya. The former is now the current president of the Agrarian Committee for the zone of Atalaya. According to complaints from community members, this group is making profit at the natives' expense: they take their lands from them and ask for clothing from Ofasa to sell to the indigenous for hens, chickens etc. A growing number of similar complaints regarding conflict between this religious group and other indigenous communities, for example the aguaruna in Imazita and river Chiriaco and the Asháninka in the Central Forest, also have to be considered.

The settlers want this conflict regarding violation of indigenous territorial rights to be seen as another problem, that of supposed 'subversion'.

In a petition signed by 77 settlers and dated 31.10.86 addressed to the OAA, they explicitly state that 'this decision to be a native community is subversive'. In an official letter. 001-86-CAJMA of 24.11.86, signed by Alejandro Trigoso Rodríguez (President of the Agrarian Committee) 'instigators who are trying to disturb the tranquillity of the settlers' are mentioned.

What is more, Mr. Duilio Lucioni Cervantes (Head of the OAA) states that 'the natives want to be native communities for opportunistic reasons'.

The majority of people in both native communities have no documentation. The birth, death and electoral registries work in such a way as to be inaccessible to them. This situation contributes to the prejudiced image that there are but a few Asháninka families from the area and the rest are from other native communities.

Conclusions

On the basis of the report and the research carried out, the existence of Tahuanti and Sabaluyo as native communities satisfying the requirements of current legislation has been established.

Asháninka refugies in the community of Poyeni

OIRA meeting in Atalaya

The native community of Tahuanti comprises 88 inhabitants covered by the census; they have Asháninka as their language and basic cultural identity, they live in a nuclear settlement on lands (covering the area between the river Tahuanti and the Mauro Quintana plot) over which they have the rights of possession and permanent use.

The native community of Sabaluyo comprises 101 inhabitants; they have Asháninka as their language and basic cultural identity, they live in a nuclear settlement on lands (covering the area between the river Chicosillo and the Camonguyo stream) over which they have the rights of possession and permanent use.

Both communities had traditional possession of the said territories long before the settlers with whom they are in conflict.

The date of native possession varies between as a minimum, 1945-52 (according to the Head of the OAA) and as a maximum 1909-1911 (according to the native elders); the settlers began to arrive in 1977, and in greater numbers between 1983-1986.

The native community cannot be blamed for the State's failure to have followed timely procedures of legal recognition and a full reorganization of territorial property in this area.

Since 1983 the Tahuanti indigenous community has suffered a more intense invasion of their farms and fallow lands, eviction from their homes and farms under production and expulsion and coercive movement from one communal area to another. They have been cooped up in a small area within their own lands and even persecuted to prevent them from 'excessive' cultivation or fishing.

All of this explains the precarious situation of instability, anxiety, malnutrition and illness which this Inspection visit found.

The native community of Sabaluyo has also been suffering the invasion of their cultivated and fallow lands, as well as exploitative actions on the part of the 'settler owners'. Because of their greater organization and communal resistance to these abuses, there is a permanent climate of tension and conflict between natives and settlers, which will lead to unforeseeable consequences.

In the face of government passivity the land conflict is escalating and moving on to higher levels of violence. There are accusations of subversion and troublemaking to try to detract from the problem, along with public threats against the lives of community members and anyone who supports them.

The conflict, again in the face of government inactivity, is spreading outside of the local arena and having an impact on national and international public and institutional opinion. If this continues, the government could be faced with a serious allegation of ethnocide from international fora.

Direct observation of the communities and study of the oral testimonies and photographs collected enables it to be noted that violations of

a number of different legal measures have been committed, and specifically violations of ILO Convention 107.

Recommendations

The DGRAAR of the Ministry of Agriculture must send a technical commission from Lima as soon as possible with the aim of demarcating the native communities Tahuanti and Sabaluyo-Mamoriari, as well as carrying out a socio-economic study of both, in which respect this report can be used as a first stage.

In doing so they will be putting in place procedures for the official recognition and titling of communal lands which, given the growing violence between the population in these areas, is urgently required.

This role cannot be taken on by, nor diverted to, the OAA or the DRA XXIII of Pucallpa, in the first case because there is evidence that they have been involved in the detected irregularities and in the second case because they have sent a technician who also supported the current neglect of the natives.

There is no time for delay, greater postponement will mean there will be no natives left in Tahuanti, they will have all left because of the pressure being put on them.

The IIP, in coordination with other public and private bodies working in the indigenous Amazonian area, can contribute to diffusion of, and training on, national and international legislation protecting indigenous rights in Atalaya, through publications, courses and other activities, aimed at the Asháninka, Piro and Shipibo populations, the settlers, State workers and population in general.

The IIP, in fulfilment of the role of protection of indigenous rights bestowed on it by Decree Law 140 and Supreme Decree 021, should continue to support both native communities until they gain their titles and in general until all of the recommendations of this report are put into effect.

The ILO must contribute to greater research and the formulation of recommendations on the different violations of Agreement 107 which fall under its sphere of responsibility. Equally, the ILO must guarantee the necessary support to enable these recommendations to be enforced and to enable the support of International Technical Cooperation.

**

Both official inspections - and a third carried out later by the Agrarian Office of Pucallpa - were equally alarmed about the magnitude of the violations of basic rights in the region.

Documents justifying the actions of government employees only served to increase these suspicions. In one department of the office of agriculture it was reaffirmed that no indigenous people existed - although 'they originally existed' - and that 'only a few refused to disappear and showed reluctance in the face of the settler presence' and that 'it was considered unlikely that they could reclaim their lands'. They put forward the solution that 'they should be hidden away to avoid problems'.

In July 1987, a first seminar on human rights was held and people young and old from more than 60 localities turned up. The reactions of the participants were disconcerting. They discovered a concept of citizenship and humanity which included them but which emphasized the pain of a whole life of injustice which they had only recently realized they were not obliged to put up with. Those running the seminar were amazed and indignant at the accumulation of violations which had occurred over a long period of time. At the mention and explanation of each of the human rights included in the Constitution, more abuses come to light.

Many of the participants complained energetically and although the complaints did not reach their destination, they created strong tensions at the regional level. Timber companies, settlers, and estate owners organized themselves into commissions to forewarn the large timber companies of Pucallpa that business was going downhill. Soon, accusations from the timber association reached Congress and the different Ministries, which spoke of agitators and subversives in Atalaya. Nevertheless, these actions were counterproductive to their interests.

What had been happening in Atalaya was only possible whilst it remained invisible. Once brought to light, no intermediate or high level authority wanted to be implicated and thus many government employees in the Pucallpa offices who undoubtedly knew, or sensed, on what basis the timber business in Atalaya had developed and who had maintained a conspiracy of silence, on being consulted by the authorities in Lima, did not dare to side with the timber companies. They even admitted that many injustices had been committed in Atalaya and that it was only through lack of economic resources that the necessary investigations had not been carried out for the suspension of some licences and forestry contracts.

There were no lack of authorities who now wanted to align themselves on the side of the indigenous. In a conversation with AIDESEP leaders and advisors the former Mayor of Atalaya explained, 'You have opened our eyes. We all thought that this was how things were, naturally, without considering what we were making these people go through. In reality, Atalaya only lives by wood and without free labour, there is no business because cattle rearing is not an activity here

but in Pucallpa. If we fulfil all the requirements you are requesting of us (salary, social security, hours etc.) Atalaya will stagnate economically. But even so, I am going to support you[7]'.

In the middle of 1987, indigenous delegates from Atalaya attended AIDESEP's General Assembly where they received the solidarity of more than thirty other indigenous organisations. In September - amidst threats and fear - the Regional Indigenous Organization of Atalaya, OIRA was established and a number of leaders from other regions helped the Asháninka of Atalaya to draw up a definitive strategy for the recovery of indigenous lands.

So AIDESEP began negotiations with the International Work Group for Indigenous affairs (IWGIA) - concerning getting support from the Danish International Aid Agency (DANIDA) for a demarcation and land titling project for Atalaya and proceeded to put pressure on the government for them to take the indigenous problems in the region seriously.

In 1988 AIDESEP and OIRA submitted an extensive report to the government, which was to be circulated internationally[8].

***

Extract from an AIDESEP report submitted to the Peruvian government in 1988

Description of the problem

Forestry problems
Timber logging is the core of regional economic activity. The estate owner, who we assume often does not have a logging contract, works on the basis of other lesser estate owners: 'contractors'.

In the Alto Ucayali, this resource is practically exhausted with the exception of the river Unini area and so the majority of logging is carried out in the Bajo Urubamba (Rivers Inuya and Sepahua). The work is carried out from March to August for the location, felling and removal and from November to January for the towing.

The search for 'labourers' is carried out on the basis of groups already previously committed and who normally have previous debts hanging over them (whose payment is even demanded with the support of the police force). The work is virtually all done by indigenous labourers, including the location of the timber itself. The payment system is through the authorization of an advance payment which they will never be able to cover, thus leaving debts for the following year.

On other occasions, the estate owner takes his 'Indians' to the forest, whole families who work as his own staff, nearly always without payment; they carry out agricultural tasks during the year and are sent to harvest during the timber season.

A third system consists of negotiating for wood already cut and taken to the bank of the stream.

In the forest, the most minimal of working conditions are not respected: twelve hour days with no more than a piece of maniok to eat, no sanitation, generally no payment, or payment well below the legal minimum. Deaths, accidents, serious aggression have all been reported in large numbers.

Tuberculosis comes from working in the forest, and is today endemic amongst a population who normaly have sufficient resources in their places of origin. It seems commonly understood in the region that this over exploitation is the only guarantee of reproduction of the system or of regional development. The indigenous population, impoverished, unregistered and illiterate, serve the system but enter into nobodies' consideration. There are no controls or defences because in reality it seems that things must continue this way in order to make economic activity in the region possible.

The depletion of forestry resources is systematic. The logging companies work in the same way on lands whether they are inhabited or not. Concretely speaking, it seems that registration or titling is avoided in order to enabl illegal logging to continue. The state of occupation of the land is never checked and the guarantee of integrity (provided for by Art. 10 of Decree Law 22175 for communities not yet titled) is impracticable. We assume that there are no controls on the origin of the wood. Nevertheless, all of these great opportunities contrast with the extreme difficulty of obtaining logging licences or contracts on the part of the indigenous communities or population. Obviously they do not know how to make the requests, but of course no government employee will give them technical support in this and promotion of such work is obviously not directed at the indigenous population. Finally, the indigenous people are swindled in terms of prices, quality, volumes and so on. In the face of aggression, deceit, unpaid work, etc., they have no authoritative body to which they can turn. There is no Land Court or Court of First Instance and the rest of the authorities clearly form an impenetrable circle.

Even the Justice of the Peace, who demands vast sums of money to write or accept accusations, is inaccessible for someone who earns a pair of trousers for a year's work.

A side effect of this is that whilst whole families are forced to go and log wood, the settlers (at a signal from the government employees) take advantage of this to invade communal indigenous lands and obtain

certificates of possession through on the spot visits organized with prior knowledge.

Accusations on the part of communities are refuted by the local government employees, who deny their existence, something which could be 'proved' if they were to visit a community which had been forced to go logging in order to cover the arrears on their interminable debts.

There exist concrete accusations regarding:

1. Failure to comply with minimum wage standards, holidays, social security and legal working days requirements (Art. 40 of Decree Law 21147).
2. Antisocial conditions of exploitation and violation of human rights of the forest workers (Art. 7 of Decree Law 21147).
3. Authorization of prior payments, as a normal form of contracting (Art. 7 of Decree Law 21147).
4. Granting of logging contracts without prior guarantees concerning indigenous territories (Art. 39 of Supreme Decree 161-77-AG and Art. 10 of Decree Law 22175).
5. Granting of exploration and logging contracts within community territories by force or through individual community members (Art 351 of Decree Law 21147).
6. Violations of the duties of the role of the staff of the Republican Guard and, of course, of the employees of the Forestry Office (Arts. 337 and 340, inc. 9 of the Penal Code).
7. Lack of attention to the priorities established by the indigenous communities in respect of logging contracts (Art 30 of Decree Law 211147)
8. Failure to comply with the minimum conditions for the granting of forestry contracts (sketches of location, feasibility studies, etc.) (Art. 33 of Supreme Decree-161-77-AG) which means that logging can be carried out in areas other than those covered by contracts (Art. 77, inc c, j, m of Decree Law 21147).
9. Absolute lack of control over the origin of wood and the inexistence of forest 'rangers' (Art. 77, inc J of Decree Law 21147; Tenth Title of Supreme Decree-161-77-AG).

This list relates only to issues which, to date, we have received complaints about and which we have information available for.

These complaints refer only to the problems in the timber logging industry which the indigenous population are faced with. The ecological disasters caused by these kinds of uncontrolled and irresponsible actions are not included amongst the complaints. The rivers Tambo and Urubamba, and particularly the Inuya and the Alto Ucayali, have all been intensively plundered since 1950, even more so since 1960, despite having been an important reserve of forestry resources. In this chain of destruction which encompasses indigenous people, small loggers or estate owners and large companies, the capital has come from the large businessmen and now, from the Agrarian Bank. In this respect, the region constitutes a short-term objective in which the future of the indigenous population is the variable with the least interest.

Land tenure
From what can be seen, the Atalaya economy can only continue its current operations through the exploitation of free or almost free indigenous labour. This explains the generalized racism and aggression towards the indigenous population, and the suppression of any attempts at organization.

Government agricultural employees are also involved as they have systematically turned a blind eye to the existence of indigenous settlements or denied their rights to occupy the land or to form communities. Strongly linked to the local power base, the government employees have encouraged invasions; detecting lands supposedly free, they have defended the invaders and have delayed requests for recognition of indigenous territories.

AIDESEP can provide official documents from Messrs. Lucioni, Vega, Guzmán and others which reflect the lack of sensitivity with regard to the indigenous problem and their interest in undermining their natural resources and the fundamentals of communal life.

Although the situation in the region can be characterized by small and medium-sized estates practising slavery and the concealment of the indigenous population, the dispute with the migrant population over land has been extremely forceful, principally since 1980, and the havoc being caused by these invasions can be observed. The bias of official bodies towards these invaders is evident. In an official report by one government employee from Region XXIII of Ucayali, it can be read that, whilst recognizing the prior existence of indigenous 'families' in particular areas of recent colonial settlement, he recommends they should move into the interior of the forest because the settlers are already working the land.

These colonial settlements are often the result of timber logging that uses temporary labourers. In nearly all cases they end up becoming an instrument of exploitation of the estate owners, and also its victims. If colonization does not increase it is not for lack of opportunities provided by the government employees. The only deterrent exists rather because of difficulties of marketing and access. In any case, on our part

(left)Miqueas Mishari, former president of AIDESEP

Indigenous assembly in Atalaya

we have been able to verify that in the region of Alto Ucayali the indigenous population has been almost completely displaced. In Bajo Urubamba, in the area of influence of the town of Atalaya (Chicosillo), invasions have reached the same level of intensity as is occurring in Sepa, with the danger that the settlers who do not gain land in Alto Urubamba may begin significant movements towards these lower areas. In Purús, with Amahuaca, Aharanahua, Culina, Cashinahua and other populations of little contact, colonization plans are being announced. In summary, it is urged that actions guaranteeing indigenous territories should be carried out, paying attention to indigenous criteria and not the vision offered by local powers and their allies in local government.

AIDESEP is negotiating a process of recognition, demarcation and titling, as well as reorganization of indigenous territories with the Ministry of Agriculture. A total of 32 communities have been highlighted for official recognition and 35 for demarcation and titling.

The record is incomplete in many ways and systematic work needs to be carried out to determine the indigenous territories, but we have had no support other than from the communities themselves and the reports of the Department of Communities in Lima. Furthermore, new requests which must be added to the list continue to arrive regularly. Furthermore, reserves, forestry, hunting, fishing and other zones have still to be determined, all of which will ensure some security for the future of the indigenous population. It is also necessary to offer alternative forms of land titling for the indigenous populations of Purús, whose special characteristics require a reserve of sufficient territory. In summary, the work of territorial rationalization must be an initial stage in the process and must involve the broad participation of the regional indigenous population.

There exist certain conditions which make this work more difficult in some ways, and which have been noted by AIDESEP's leaders and trainers.

* The economic and occupational dependence of the indigenous population, which is the result of the described system of exploitation and displacement, means that many communities remain abandoned or with few inhabitants over long periods of time. The mestizos benefit from this - sometimes forewarned by the government employees themselves - by irreversibly invading the lands. Many families, entire communities even, are thus held on the estate and, on other occasions, once an owner has established himself, they become the basis for a new estate and the consequent denial of the community by government employees. Any 'escapes', which are dangerous and suppressed, result in displacement to distant places and temporary abandonment of the traditional settlement.

* The reduction in essential living space to which many indigenous communities and family groups are subjected is also at the root of clashes. The repression and criminal activity resulting from these clashes are also the motive for 'flight' in the face of a system which will never find justice in favour of the indigenous population. Similarly, when a community lacks the most basic resources for survival, the temporary disintegration of the community occurs, along with the need to search for work with estate owners and timber companies.

* Obligatory or forced clashes between members of different ethnic groups, in particular the Asháninka and Piro, brought about by the estate owners in order to capture children and labourers, have caused resentment which, apart from hindering the process of indigenous demands, which necessarily requires unity to succeed, causes clashes and community divisions and, unfortunately, in some cases, support for a process of territorial invasion on the part of the indigenous population themselves.

* The generalized practice of giving the same name to a number of people who are the subjects of a single estate owner, which in itself can bring about serious racist connotations, in many cases facilitates the negative attitude of the local government official towards recognizing the communal territory as, according to him, it consists of 'only one family'.

* Another current practice is that of granting individual certificates of possession to natives with the idea that they offer security over the lands. When a conflict occurs it is argued that it is a dispute between settlers and that the indigenous owner of the land has renounced the notion of community member. What is worse, when some members of the community cede rights to a temporary occupier through economic pressures, it is claimed that a sale between individuals has occurred, thus resolving the problem.

These factors, together with other practices observed, such as marriage to mestizos etc., are all used to their advantage by the government officials in order to spread a generalized image of community decomposition which favours their interests (since, of course, the transfer of licences, sales and purchases, certificates of possession ... etc. are all more profitable for them than the consolidation of stable indigenous territories).

Concretely, AIDESEP has received complaints and accusations regarding the following aspects:

* A negative attitude within the Ministry of Agriculture's offices on receiving documents; up to little more than one year ago it was not easy for an indigenous person to even gain entry to the offices. The employees have argued that there were formal defects in the documents, ignoring their obligation to provide guidance in these cases.

* Systematic lack of attention to requests for recognition, titling or extension. There even exist some cases of encouragement of urgent occupations of lands requested by indigenous people on the part of settlers; in cases where land has already been requested, which demonstrates a knowledge of the indigenous occupation on the part of the government officials, forestry contracts have been granted (or logging activity permitted), making fulfilment of the State commitment to respect the integrity of communal territories impossible.

* Invasions of lands titled, requested or occupied by indigenous people, with the knowledge of government officials.

* Situations of slavery, physical mistreatment and kidnapping against an indigenous labour force living in denigrating conditions of servitude on at least 17 estates, whose conditions should have brought about their appropriation a long time ago.

* Systematic buying and selling of lands in the face of the total passivity of government officials. There are posters all over the place announcing the sale of lands. Speculation is one of the main motives of colonization, one of the consequences of its productive failure, one of the explanations of the indifference of the government officials in the face of titling of communities and the worst enemy of the indigenous people who, unlike the immigrants, need the territory on a long-term basis for their livelihood, social and cultural reproduction.

* Granting of certificates of possession without prior verification of the real occupiers. Whilst the path to recognition of indigenous land rights is a long and difficult one, it is easy to obtain certificates of ownership for anyone who wants to obtain credit with the Agrarian Bank. In turn, the commitment of a forthcoming credit becomes an insurmountable obstacle in the recuperation of usurped indigenous lands.

* Collusion between different authorities with the aim of seizing territories. There are complaints of the appointment of a police authority in territories occupied by communities or indigenous families or in adjacent zones, thus authorizing the obligation of people to work on the lands of the said authority or the lands seized by it.

It is equally common for agrarian conflicts to be solved through 'agreements' with the Justice of the Peace, who is the only legal authority in the area. Agreements which never involve the slightest justice for the indigenous population.

This bias on the part of the government officials, which prevents any administrative agreement being reached (and whose superior offices in Pucallpa or Satipo, are inaccessible for any indigenous person from the region), obliges recourse to the Justice of the Peace and the Political Authorities for 'arranged' solutions to many land conflicts. Despite the fact that these authorities have changed a number of times since AIDESEP first started working in the area, their position has always been to support their own and not the indigenous population.

* In cases where a titling process has been forced through, the areas offered have been minimal and requests for extension have not been considered; the criteria highlighted in Art. 10 of Decree Law 22175 are not taken into consideration; neither are those in Art. 14 of the text of Convention 107 of the ILO.

The described situation details, very superficially, the current land tenure situation and is based on observations during visits to the area by AIDESEP leaders and on complaints received from the people.

Situation regarding people's rights

This is the most worrying aspect of the problem, since the human being is central to civil society.

The gravity of the situation stems from the extreme racism and aggressive discrimination which encourages the treatment of indigenous people as an inferior race, despite being the original inhabitants and ancestral owners of all these lands. The human rights violations are so brutal and so common that, whilst they alarm any visitor (as could be seen from the official reports of the Peruvian Indigenous Institute and the Work Inspectorate), they do not touch the sensitivities of the mestizo population nor do they seem out of place to the local authorities.

500 years on, the indigenous population of this region continue to be viewed from the same perspective as that of the Spanish conquistadors.

The majority of work relationships can be defined as slavery and the remainder are based on servitude. It is a current practice to take children away from their parents and keep them as perpetual slaves through a strange 'right of baptism'. The system of perpetual indebtedness links a person and his or her descendants to an estate owner for life. In the partially frustrated inspection of the Ministry of Labour various cases were noted of children who were taken to an estate at the age of 10 or 12 and today, at 50, are still working there and are punished if they try to escape. They receive no payment except maybe a few clothes. For the magistrates and the police this seems perfectly normal and people such as Castilla or Laws such as 15037 or the Agrarian Reform or the different measures of the State Constitution are still not known in the area.

With regard to labour laws in particular, there is not one measure which is respected and despite the fact that any of these practices would have served as justification for the appropriation of estates or the withdrawal of forestry contracts, the accumulation of offences, including a lack of respect for life and the physical integrity of the 'Indians' belonging to each estate owner, it is this situation which gains respect from society and the local authorities.

Furthermore, there are many indigenous people without identification, not even within a census, without birth certificates, with no documentation and no name, despite a number of attempts being made in this respect recently.

The role of the State in the protection of all human, civil and working rights is ignored. At a local level, this is because of the benefit to local power groups. Outside of Atalaya it is because the State is inaccessible to the indigenous population under normal circumstances. Apart from which, there are still no people trained in this respect. The Court of First Instance, for work or land issues, is based in Pucallpa, Tarma, Huánuco or Satipo, places whose distance would incur impossible costs for the indigenous people.

The possibility of defence, in the current state of affairs, can only come from their own organizational capacity and indigenous solidarity. The State will only be able to help through a decisive reorganization of its local structures and bold action in support of the fulfilment of the Law, the Constitution and other international agreements.

Any visit will corroborate the number and severity of violations of the most basic human rights. Cases such as the following have been reported to AIDESEP:

- Slavery (the most frequent form of working relationship; there are 17 estates already accused of having permanent work relationships based on slavery, but there exist many other types of temporary relationship which, although considered as employment agreements, result in antisocial forms of exploitation). Given this situation, it must be understood that other lesser labour offences are also current practice: absence of a payroll, minimum working hours (normally 6 until 6), Sunday work, holidays, social security, minimum health and safety standards (community members relate how a labourer was executed during logging work because he had fractured a femur; during their visits, AIDESEP directly experienced the case of a young labourer whose body was left on the beach; finally, young workers with permanent disabilities are obliged to 'sort out' their derisory payments with the Judge, payments which later never materialize and cannot be demanded). Work on the part of minors, children of the indebted labourers, is compulsory.

- Kidnapping and abduction of minors, either directly or through 'baptisms' in order to maintain them in a permanent situation of servitude without payment in the urban surrounds of Atalaya or on the estates (as 'servants'). Regarding the conditions in which these minors are held, it should be noted that in the first two cases in which the freedom of minors was achieved, one showed serious signs of starvation and bruising on the body and the other died a few hours after having been taken from the home of his 'godmother', the victim of a beating.

- Debtors' prison: this is a current occurrence on the estates, backed up by permanent threats from the authorities for those who escape. On occasions, the police reaction is also one of repression of those who escape. Relationships prohibited by the Forestry Law are widely practised, such as advance payments and debt bondage, which are no more than ways of covering up systems of slavery.

- Obstacles to free movement: the Sepa Penal Colony is an obstacle to the movement of the indigenous population, who cannot reason with the whims of the staff of this prison and their timber company friends.

- 'Agreed' rape of minors, for small payments

- Violations of the right to life: dead or disappeared labourers are numerous.

- Violations of physical integrity: there are numerous complaints of torture, whippings, head cropping, mutilation, permanent invalidity, etc. AIDESEP attempted to cure a youth of 16 who had been permanently blinded by blows from a machete because he refused to harvest yucca when his feet were covered in cuts and after a twelve hour day.

- Against the right of petition, on occasions not even allowing entry to an indigenous person into the particular offices, nor acknowledging their demands in departmental reports

- Against the right of property, not only of their age-old territories and natural resources but of belongings and produce. The community

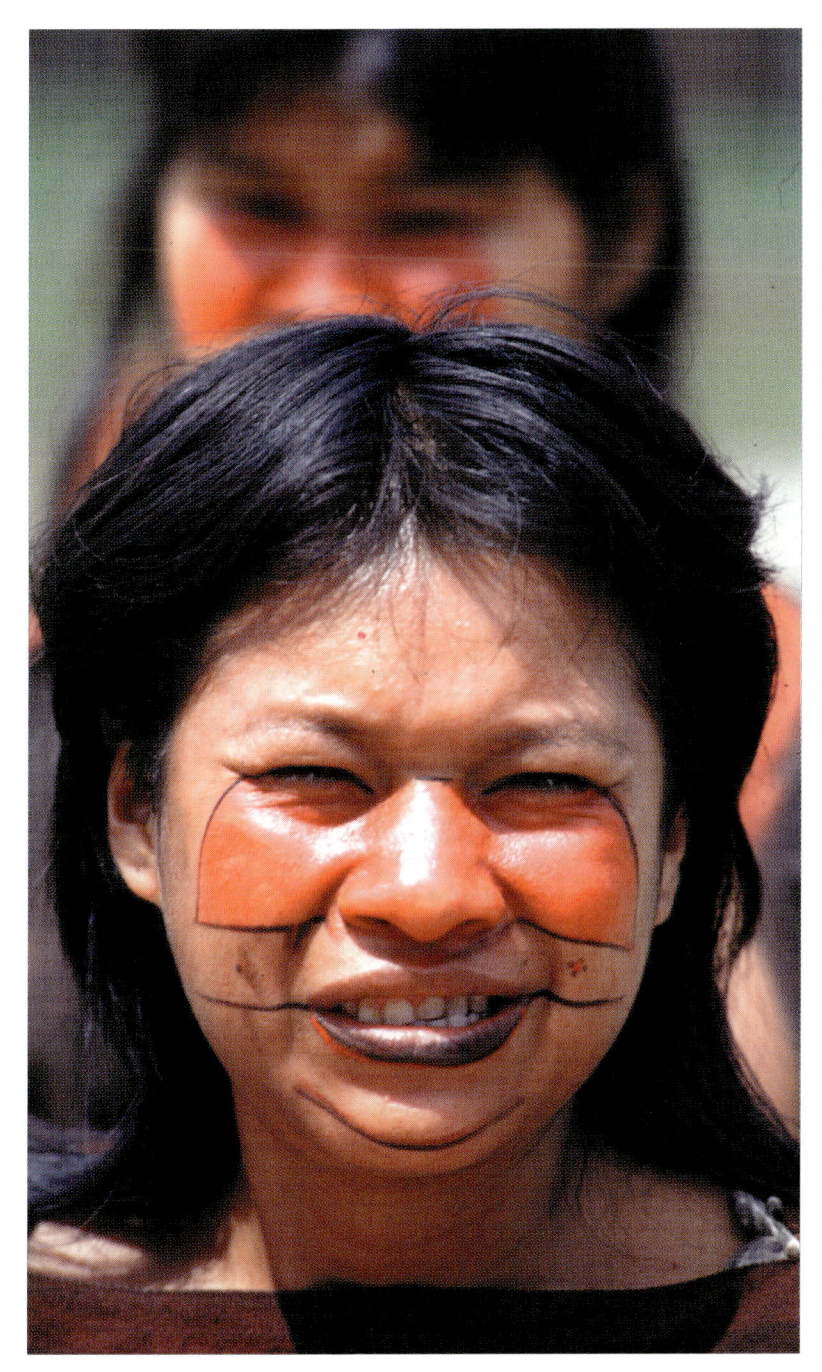

members bring their wood down to the river and it is then not recognized as theirs, there is confiscation of agricultural produce (in the Sepa), dispossession of motors provided as payment for 30 years work, etc.

-Racial discrimination: in public offices, in the actions of the authorities etc. Every statement collected is a demonstration of the disdain with which the native inhabitants are considered - as inferior beings, unproductive, incapable, etc.

-Violations of homes, sometimes with the aim of collecting servants.

- Denial of their own name, often in order to homogenize and distinguish the staff attached to any one estate. Thus it can be said, 'he is a Campos, he belongs to Pinedo'.

This is only a short summary of the aggressions observed and denounced during our visits. Other rights which the indigenous people are refused could of course be added to the list: the right to well being and family security, the right to an education and their own culture, the minimum right to a good state of health, the impossibility of exercising constitutional guarantees, etc.

***

The impact of the report was substantial, both at government level and abroad. The central government was concerned about the gravity of such accusations and the repercussions that an international complaint based on such an anachronistic offence as that of slavery in a modern and democratic country[9] could have. In this instance, pressure from international bodies such as the ILO was very effective; a warning that they were aware of the situation was sufficient to have effect.

On 21st October 1988, the government issued an unprecedented resolution (Ministerial Resolution 0083-88-PCM). The existence of serious violations of the human rights of the indigenous population of the region of Atalaya was noted, which required the creation of a Multi Sectoral Commission of the highest level to remedy the situation. This was made up of the Deputy Minister for Social Promotion, the Director General of Justice, the Director General for Agrarian Reform, the Director General for Labour and the Head of the Peruvian Indigenous Institute.

The final report of the Commission is dramatic. It can be summed up in one sentence: slavery is a fact in Atalaya. We here reproduce extracts from the report.

***

Extracts from the Final Report on the measures referring to the rights, well being and development of the ethnic natives of the Atalaya region

In accordance with the relevant resolution, the Commission submits this final report to the President of the Council of Ministers, in which urgent measures are analysed and proposed in order to contribute to overcoming the problem existing in the conflict zone.

General characteristics of the area

The area of conflict is situated in the province of Atalaya, district of Ucayali, covering the micro-region between the estuary of the river Sepahua in Bajo Urubamba, up to the river Unine on the borders of Gran Pajonal, the valleys of Inuya and of Alto Purús and the community of Betijay in Alto Ucayali.

Strategic, geographic and other reasons could lead the area of conflict to be increased or reduced, given that the neighbouring zones (Purús, river Tambo, Bajo Urubamba, Gran Pajonal), have similar historical, geographic and social conditions and could demonstrate the same problems as those in the stated micro-region. According to the national population census, the area in concern has a population of 12,400 inhabitants, with a clear majority - equivalent to 76% of the total population - living in rural areas (National Institute of Statistics (INE) National Census 1981).

The region of Atalaya is a strategic area of our Amazon, both for its geopolitical location and for its natural resources since, once the Puerto Prado-Atalaya highway - which will link it with Satipo - is built, it will become the closest area of low forest land to Lima and neighbouring departments: similarly, it would provide the possibility of integrating the border zones of Purús and Yurúa both administratively and economically, thus achieving contact with the native populations and safeguarding current borders, as well as being able to benefit from the wealth of forest and soil resources.

The town of Atalaya, capital of the province, shows the scarce presence of a governmental system, which leaves the path clear, in contrast, for the local power group, which is based on the stockpiling of the produce of extractive and agricultural activities, as well as the control of the transport and marketing of consumer goods.

The rural population is largely made up of a significant indigenous population - conditioned to the status of cheap or free labour, both as workers in the logging industry and labourers on the estates - small farmers or extractors and servants, completely dependent on and dominated by the estate owners and their intermediaries, whose excesses crudely reproduce the traditional exploitation system of the Amazon, leading to land conflicts, as well

as a series of situations of open violation of the human and employment rights of the natives.

This reality, which has been experienced and analysed by the Inter-Ethnic Association for Development of the Peruvian Rainforest, AIDESEP, led to complaints being lodged with a number of governmental organisms (Public Prosecutor's Office, Judicial Authorities, Ministries of the Interior, Employment, Agriculture, Justice and Presidency), as well as with the ILO, an international body which acknowledged the complaint, informing our Foreign Office and Ministry of Employment and Social Promotion officially.

In May 1988, the Ministry of Employment, in coordination with the Peruvian Indigenous Institute, carried out a special inspection of the zone in order to verify the alleged irregularities and to impose corresponding sanctions on aspects within its competence. The participation of other public sectors was negotiated and the partial support of the Ministry of Defence and of the Interior gained; participation of the Ministry of Agriculture was not achieved.

During the inspection visit, some of the farming estates accused of debt bondage and slavery were visited. This enabled confirmation of the truth of the said accusations. Nevertheless, the study could not be carried out in any depth due to a lack of collaboration on the part of the local authorities and the fact that the accused estate owners were absent or chose to hide once they heard of the presence of the Commission, leaving only the natives maintained in their service. This absence suggested a guilty conscience from the start.

The Native Communities

In the province of Atalaya there is an indigenous population of approximately 5,000 inhabitants belonging to different ethno-linguistic groups such as the Asháninka, commonly known as 'Campas'. Shipibo-conibos, Piros, Amahuacas and Yaminahuas, all make up approximately 80 native communities, of which 23 are officially registered, 17 with titled territories and 40 with neither recognition or titling.

The native population of this area live in two types of settlement; 'free' communities and 'captive' communities. The former maintain a certain amount of autonomy over how their community and its resources are managed, whilst this is not to deny the socio-economic mechanisms of domination and ethnic oppression of which they are victims. This causes them to have serious land problems, through permanent invasion by estate owners, holders of logging concessions and settlers onto their communal territories, who excessively exploit all of the communities' resources amidst the insufficiency of farming land, thus causing the breakdown of the community unit and the tacit threat to their ethnic integrity.

The 'captive' communities are those whose ancestral lands have been seized and who find themselves not only robbed but subjected to servitude within medium and large-sized farming estates or by logging companies, forming a free or semi-free labour force whose employers reduce them to the condition of permanent labourers with no capacity for making use of their goods or even of their own lives under the mechanism of the system of advance payments or debt bondage. Servitude which, in many cases, has the marked characteristics of slavery and which has led the very exploiters to state with bare-faced pride, 'it is not the State that makes the laws here, it is the bosses'.

The necessary demographic statistics for these communities are not available. Nevertheless, the account of estates on which native staff work, submitted to the Commission by the Mayor of Atalaya, may serve as an indicator, in which 47 estates are mentioned, of which 17 have been accused of human rights violations, with slavery and servitude being the basis on which work relationships are founded.

This situation of oppression and dependence is forced on the indigenous population, in spite of their being the original inhabitants and ancestral owners of the said lands, due to the minimal role of the State. Its absence in the zone allows the hegemony of local power groups. Out of this situation, and the need for self-defence, out of the indigenous people's own solidarity, was born OIRA, the Regional Indigenous Organization of Atalaya, initially composed of 25 native communities, being the organized natives themselves who confronted the situation of injustice and subjugation in which they found themselves, in order to create an awareness of their rights and to gain ethnic respect at a national level. They consider it necessary to strengthen coordinating relations between the State and Native Organizations who put themselves in the situation of brave spokes people for the formulation and implementation of all action plans.

An analysis of the problem

The land

Invasion of lands and colonization
- A growing flow of settlers already taking possession of the banks of the main rivers, causing the invasion of territories titled or occupied by native populations, many of which are recognized as native communities, violating the guarantees of these latter which are provided for by law.

- A usual mechanism for carrying out invasions of native lands is to take advantage of the temporary displacement caused by the logging encampments in order to claim that the invaded lands were unoccupied. The same argument is used with regard to lands at rest or 'fallow' which the native communities, in accordance with the ecological demands of the Amazon, continue to respect ancestrally.

Over the whole area in question, there is no Land Court, and so conflicts of tenure are 'resolved' by the Justice of the Peace, always in favour of the local power group.

There exist in the region colonization programmes which are underway (for example, 'Inuya'), or planned (Purús), which lack any actions aimed at recognizing and registering native communities. This means that they may be making use of areas that should be held for the benefit of communities yet to be recognized.

The growing demographic burden which colonization puts on the region by way of a population which over exploits resources, will lead to a future 'ecocide'.

Titling

There exist a large number of communities which have yet to be registered and/or titled. This means that the measures of the Law of Native Communities - which declares that the State guarantees the rights of native communities to their territories by putting in place the corresponding Land Registry and that it is not necessary for communities to request titling - are not being fulfilled.

Certificates of possession are being granted to individuals with no prior verification of the pre-existing tenure and ownership of the land, meaning that settlers are being given land which has been traditionally occupied by natives or, worse still, lands which are titled in the name of a community.

Certificates of possession are granted on an individual basis to natives who form part of groups likely to be recognized as a community, thus ruling out the possibility of communal titling guaranteed by law and encouraging community disintegration.

The procedure used to determine the amount of land to be titled does not follow realistic criteria, and so the area granted ends up being insufficient to guarantee the normal socio-economic development of the community.

This causes numerous requests for territorial enlargement which the natives attempt to alleviate their lack of land with.

The process established for titling of native communities is long and complicated, in contrast with the ease with which certificates of possession can be obtained, which is the normal form of legalising occupations of land by settlers.

The employees of the Agrarian Office of Atalaya do not begin to process the complaints or claims submitted by the natives (recognition), titling, enlargement, invasion, etc.). Often they will not even acknowledge their files, and thus there remains no proof of their processing, transgressing current legal mechanisms, in particular Art. 23 of Decree Law 22175 which states that government officials and employees should give priority attention to communities, with this responsibility to do so falling under civil and criminal law.

Similarly, the staff of the said Agrarian Office are frequently accused of colluding with the invaders of communal lands, systematically ignoring the existence of indigenous settlements or denying them their rights to property and to constitute a community.

The Forestry Problem

- Granting of logging contracts to third persons within territories occupied by or titled to ethnic groups or assigned for their use, ignoring Art. 35 of Decree Law 21147, which provides that within the native communities' territories, extractive measures can only be carried out by them. Similarly, the granting of contracts and licences is carried out in a discriminatory manner, denying the natives the possibility of obtaining them, contradicting the priority which should be given to native communities in the concession of forestry contracts (Art. 30 of Decree Law 21147).

Logging is currently the main activity in the region and it is carried out through the mechanism of a chain of intermediaries (logging company - or estate owner -, paymasters and sub-paymasters) which ends with the participation of the natives. This system contradicts that which is laid out in Art. 7 of Decree Law 21147, in which all types of advance payments are prohibited, unless controlled or supervised by the competent bodies.

There exist wood merchants and paymasters plying the rivers who stockpile large quantities of wood to later sell in Pucallpa without it being clear how they justify where it has come from, for nobody can sell wood without having a forestry contract which authorizes its marketing (Decree Law 21147).

The ambiguous current regulations regarding the granting of forestry contracts enables the possibility of the existence of a series of abuses, with serious ecological and socio-economic consequences, since logging concessions for areas up to 5,000 hectares are granted by the local district forestry office, which is generally run by a technician; authorization for up to 10,000 hectares is granted by the Pucallpa departmental office and only if it is more than 10,000 hectares does it go to the National Office, as a prior technical requirement.

Progressive destruction of the tropical rain forest eco-system is occurring, along with a plundering which is leading to the extinction of the most valuable species of wood, with excessive logging and lack of fulfilment of the measures on reforestation, and without even the presence of the authorities to caution fulfilment.

The work conditions in the logging encampments violate regulations on the labour rights of workers, as well as attacking fundamental human rights, with advance payments or debt bondage being the established form of work for extractive activity.

- Unpunished robbery of wood and fraudulent transactions are mechanisms frequently used against the natives. In one particular case, the communities neighbouring the Sepa Penal Colony accused members of the police force working there of seizing their wood, having received no orders from the competent authority, with the aim of marketing the wood for their own benefit. Thus whilst dedicating themselves to being the timber 'middlemen', benefiting from their investiture to commit crimes against those in their pay.

The Labour Problem

The natives' working conditions on the farming estates and in the logging encampments demonstrate inhuman characteristics, as is indicated by the accusations against 17 estates, partially verified in all their gravity during the inspection carried out by the Commission that was sent to the area in May 1988 by the Ministry of Employment and the Peruvian Indigenous Institute.

On the said estates, even when the workers have not been recruited through means of abduction or buying and selling, the conditions under which they carry out their tasks are such that they verge on slavery.

We can summarize the normal working day on the estates and in the logging encampments which work with the natives as follows:

Ways of recruiting labour

On the estates there exists a population which remains there from generation to generation, the servile condition being passed down from father to son and whose origins can be found in the incursions of the first half of this century; obliging women and children to work as servants all their life.

The violent abduction of children is frequent, or their kidnapping under cover of the sponsorship of baptism in order to keep them as permanent servants, both on the estates and in the houses of the employers or other mestizo residents of Atalaya, even in their relatives' homes in Pucallpa and Lima. The supposed baptism is used as a form of psychological blackmail over the native who can rarely gain access to legal documentation, such as birth certificates, voter registration cards and so on. The employer holds the certificate of baptism and with this, the entire life of the native.

Workers who have not been recruited by these methods are recruited via the different method of advance payments or debt bondage. In this method, the employer ensures the labour of a particular person and his entire family in agricultural activity or extractive activities by giving him an advance payment of a certain sum of money and/or providing tools, supplies - clothes or a service such as health care - which have to be reimbursed or paid back by the workers at a cost calculated by the employer, that is to say, a high one, tying the native to the employer until the debt is paid. In this way, a large debt which cannot be paid back is generated, leaving the whole family subjected to interminable exploitation, and additional physical-sexual abuses on the part of the employer. Under this system of exploitation, entire families are held under the threat of being imprisoned for unpayable and permanent debts, which, judging by the complaints, has the support of the police and judicial authorities.

On being subjected and subjugated violently under working conditions based on the alienation of their free will, the natives find themselves immersed in a system of slavery, deprived of all liberty as well as of their constitutional rights.

Working conditions

This whole system of human exploitation, which in many cases is being aggravated by the presence of drug traffickers and terrorists in the area, violates constitutional principles and standards, human rights and legal measures which govern employment relations, measures aimed at protecting minors and women.

The law is being violated in the following ways:

Salaries

The concept of a salary or daily wage has no legal effect in the area. The employer grants a form of payment, under the so-called method of advance payment, making the payment in kind (food, clothes, tools, utensils etc.) at overvalued prices in relation to the regional market, causing the worker to accumulate a continual series of 'advances' from the employer, in such a way that the work obligation becomes permanent and unending, violating legal measures: Supreme Decree No. 0006-71 of 29.11.71 and Law No. 6871 on salaries.

The Working Day

It was possible to verify that legal stipulations with regard to the 48 hour working week and 8 hour working day provided for in Art. 44 of the State Constitution, along with the 45 hour working week for women and children, in accordance with Laws 2851 and 4239 were not being fulfilled. The natives work 10 or 12 hours a day, the fact that they are not paid a minimum living wage only making matters worse, before even considering that they should be paid overtime.

Weekly rest and Sunday payments
As a consequence of the above, the native worker gains no rest on a Sunday, let alone rest or remuneration for bank holidays, which is not in accordance with Law No. 10908, Decree Law 21106, Supreme Decree of 27.04.49.

Holidays
Throughout the Atalaya region, employers ignore the legal duty to grant holiday to their workers. This is not in accordance with the legal measures of Law No. 13683 and Supreme Decree 24.10.61 with regard to paid holidays. No physical rest periods exist, nor additional compensation for working throughout the time which should correspond to holiday for the year worked.

Social benefits and compensatory payments for length of service
The social rights or the right to compensatory payments for each year in an employer's service is denied the natives. On the part of the workers, the virtual or total ignorance of their rights or the paltry salary that they may receive in cash does not enable them to try to claim their rights because the possible departments which could deal with their claims are situated too far from the zone. This leads to a failure to comply with Articles 42, 43, 44, 47 and 57 of the State Constitution.

Social Security
The lack of implementation on the part of the employers of legal measures with reference to the registration of payrolls of employees, employer registers, pay slips, and the non-payment of legal salaries is also due to the non-existence of registers with the Peruvian Social Security (IPSS); thus the native working population is prevented from accessing benefits such as sickness, maternity, disability, work accident or any other allowance likely to be provided by the law (Law 22482, Decree Law 19990, Decree Law 20604).

Occupational health
The existence or the provision of safety implements which employers should provide for their workers, such as rubber boots, helmets, gloves etc., is unknown. This means that the native workers find themselves, besides the dangers that working in the jungle already implies, exposed to greater risks from work accidents.

Accidents that do happen are either treated out of their own pocket or, if dealt with by the employer, are added to the natives' account; in cases of invalidity, these people are generally abandoned.

On the estates and in the encampments there is strict control through the use of private police, any resistance or violation of the existing system is punished with physical reprisals or with a period in the cells. If a worker escapes, the employer has the right to look for the person and bring him or her back by force (with police help), arguing that there are debts outstanding. There were many complaints regarding this.

The Regional Work Zone of Atalaya
No Work Sector authority or employment forum exists in the region to whom the workers' problems can be put and resolved. Labour conflicts are resolved by the Sub-Prefect or the Justice of the Peace, who have both been accused of showing open partiality in favour of the employers.

The Problem of Human Rights
According to the different accusations received, human rights violations are being carried out against the natives in a number of different ways:

Against the right to life and physical integrity
Accusations of torture, mutilation and unpunished assassinations against native labourers were received.

Abduction of women and children.

Sexual abuse of minors and married adults.

The fact that the natives have dared denounce the prevailing situation in Atalaya to the central government is causing a series of reprisals on the part of the accused, expressed through physical aggression (suffered by the President of OIRA, Mauro Salazar) and through death threats received by the leaders Miqueas Mishari Mofat, AIDESEP leader, Miguel Camaiteri of the Asháninka Organization of Gran Pajonal and Oswaldo Castro, OIRA advisor.

Racial discrimination
The mestizos of the area are accustomed to openly declaring that the natives are not human beings, thus justifying their abuse of them.

They ignore their real names, calling entire populations by the employer's surname and a first name chosen at random by this latter, denying them the right to choose their own names.

Slavery and servitude.

Attendance of the children at school is prevented or made difficult, occasionally being allowed up to a certain age.

The desire to prevent the registration of natives, with the consequent denial and destruction of birth certificates and other identity documents.

Against the right of property
Violent invasion of their lands by employers, settlers and loggers.
Theft of their forestry resources as well as construction materials.

Against their liberty
Impossibility or difficulty of free movement outside the estate or encampment, and difficulty of receiving visitors inside the same.

In the Sepa control lodge, undocumented natives are often hampered in their movements along the river Urubamba, only permitting them to continue their journey on payment of a sum of money.

Violation of homes, with the aim of abducting servants or capturing 'debtors'.

Imprisonment for non-payment of debts, with the knowledge of the local authorities, in improvised cells on the estates, with the threat of being sent to prison.

Against the right to request justice
Claims from natives not being acknowledged and/or even accepted by some State offices.

All contact with agents of the public services, with publicity and with strangers in general is made difficult, hiding or denying the existence of the native population on the estates. Doctors from the 'Central Forest' health project, funded by Save the Children Fund, Peru from Great Britain relate that the estate owners refused to allow them free entry onto the estates, only permitting them to see the young and adult men who made up the work force and not the women and children and so it could not be estimated exactly how many children existed on the estates.

It is worth noting that the political, police and judicial authorities are all accused of collusion with the employers and of active participation in the abuse.

Conclusions
The Commission's work has enabled enough evidence to be collected to consider that the situation in the Atalaya region is effectively an attack on national legislation, and one which practically constitutes a picture of ethnocide, since it is the native population which is the most affected by it, and it merits urgent action on the part of the State.

The following recommendations must give rise to a series of actions whose initiative and control demand the establishment of a coordinating body in which the native organizations affected must have a place (AIDESEP, OIRA and others).

It is proposed that the Multi Sectoral Commission is extended by Resolution of the Prime Minister and participation of the Development Corporation of Ucayali, the Directorate-General of Forestry and Fauna of the Ministry of Agriculture, the Episcopal Conference and the Indigenous Organizations AIDESEP and OIRA should be included.

For the functioning of the said Commission, contact with the ILO is recommended, whose intervention may provide funds to cover the costs that will be generated. Furthermore the said Commission must provide regular reports to the Prime Minister and a General Report on the progress of immediate actions six months of its establishment, on the basis of which medium term actions will be defined as well as the organism or organisms responsible for their implementation and control

With reference to the problem of land and forestry resources

* That the Special Control Commission requires information from Departmental Agrarian Units (UAD) XXIII and XVI on:
- number of native communities registered, titled or in the process of such, with their location and size.
- information on settler estates, indicating location, size and adjoining areas.
- information on the number of current licences and/or logging contracts, indicating area, species, volumes, location and duration.

* That the Atalaya Agrarian Bank provides information on the total credits granted for agricultural and livestock production in the zone corresponding to the 87 and 88 agricultural years: including those granted to native communities and/or indigenous organizations, association or individuals.

* That ENCI (Empresa Nacional de Comercialización de Insumos - National Marketing Board) provides information on the farmers and native communities which provided agricultural products and their respective volumes for the years 87 and 88.

* That Departmental Agrarian Units XXIII and XVI suspend all further allocation of contract concessions or licences for forestry extraction in the Atalaya area, with the consequent halting of all processing in this respect, at the risk of being prosecuted under criminal law, until recognition, titling and reorganization of the native communities has been accomplished.

* Once the required information on land tenure in the area has been provided, the Commission must carry out the necessary reviews and checks to detect irregularities that have occurred and determine the required methods, in terms of:
    - Stockpiling of land and unauthorized transactions.
    - Verification of direct management.
    - Land invasions and provision of certificates of possession and forestry contracts on community territories already titled or to be titled.
    - Failure to comply with labour regulations on the different agricultural lands and in the forestry extraction centres.

* That a forestry police be established in the area, and that until this is in operation, agreement be reached with OIRA so that they may represent the indigenous authorities, with forest ranger responsibilities in coordination with the Local Police. This implies the need for training of a native forestry police force.

* Application of the Forestry Tax in Atalaya to the benefit of the native communities, whose forestry resources have been plundered.

* That the implementation of the agreement between OIRA, AIDESEP and the Ministry of Agriculture be speeded up, with the aim of completing the recognition and titling of the native communities in the region of Atalaya.

* That on the basis of this report, the Prime Minister processes a Supreme Decree on the Ethnic Territorial Reserves of the Amazon, giving priority to the micro-region of Atalaya in order to guarantee and preserve the ecological balance of the zone and avoid dispossession of the land of the native communities.

With reference to employment rights

* Immediate fulfilment of the pending re-registration of the estates visited during the inspection carried out by the Ministry of Employment in May 1998, and widening of the corresponding sanctions in the case of their not having taken the corrective measures ordered by the former.

* Inspection of a preventive nature of all the other estates and logging encampments working with natives in the region, which should be carried out on a multi-sectoral basis.

* Creation of an Atalaya Regional Work Zone, whose inspection service must be adequately provided for (river transportation, radiotelephony etc.) and in which there are included native assistants, trained in labour laws.

* Coordination with native organizations for the permanent training of communal authorities and leaders in the area of labour law and constant dissemination of labour standards, through leaflets, chats, radio etc. Preferably in native language.

* Creation of an office of the Peruvian Indigenous Institute in Atalaya, to ensure the defence of the native populations and to carry out the roles of research and coordination of the work of the other public and private institutions dealing with native populations.

With reference to human rights

* The establishment of a permanent Court of the First Instance and a Provincial Director of Public Prosecutions, based in Atalaya.

* The urgent appointment of an ad-hoc Ombudsman to investigate the complaints received regarding human rights violations and to initiate the necessary criminal proceedings.

* Establishment of guarantees for the personal safety of the native informants, as well as for the leaders, advisors and other people who have had death threats over the past few months.

* Establishment of a free legal advice office based in Atalaya, which would be financed through the support and coordination of the AIDE-MIN-JUS-DGJ-Popular Legal Offices agreement of the Ministry of Justice.

* Definition and emphasis of the operative role of the Police Force as guarantor of the safeguard of human rights of the natives.

* That training programmes be developed for the native population around the issues of Civil and Human Rights, through an agreement with OIRA, AIDESEP, the Ministry of Justice and the Public Prosecutor's Office.

* That an agreement be established between the National Institute of Statistics (INE), the Electoral Register and the Town Hall of Atalaya in order to complete the registration and documentation of the native population and the opening of Registry Offices in a greater number of native communities.

* Intervention on the part of the National Council for Children and the Family, through its Technical Secretariat in order to safeguard the rights and social interests of families and children who are possible victims of abuse.

* Intervention of the Office for the Defence of Women's Rights of the Ministry of Justice, in support of women who may have suffered threats or other at the hands of the estate owners and employers.

* Change of the legal jurisdiction of Huánuco to Ucayali, based in Pucallpa, since the province of Atalaya depends legally on Huánuco.

* At a national level, appointment of a special Ombudsman for the defence of the rights of native communities.

With reference to Public Bodies

* Reorganization of the existing Public Offices in the Atalaya region, directed towards more effective and coordinated action to the benefit of the native populations, with the consequent removal or relocation of authorities and officials who have not fulfilled their roles, initiating the corresponding administrative procedures against them.

* That in the Atalaya Agrarian Office a department for native communities is created: an office to deal with native issues, staffed by native people.

* Definition and creation of joint ways of working between all of the existing public organisms in order to guarantee a coordinated effort on behalf of the native communities.

   - Strengthening of the government budgets in order to achieve the above objectives.
   - Strict control of the fulfilment of Art. 21 of the Law of Native Communities regarding priority actions by the different public institutions on behalf of the native population.

* Carry out studies on the situation of the adjoining areas, Yurúa, Purús, Gran Pajonal, river Mishahua, on which there is little information.

* Coordination with private, state and international bodies which have technical and financial resources and which may be able to provide support to these actions, such as ENAC (Empresa Nacional de la Coca), Pichis Palcazú Project, MINPECO (Minero Peru Comercial), UNFDAC (UN Fund for Drug Abuse Control), ILO, UNICEF, etc.

* This commission will make contact with the corresponding public entities, in order that they immediately commence the actions recommended in this report.

For the Multi-Sectoral Commission:

President:
Dr. Domingo Treneman Gonzales
Ing. Hector Torreblanca Cruz
Vice Minister for Social Promotion
Director General of Agrarian Reform and AR
Dr Luis R Corvetto Cabrera
Director General of Justice
Dr Jesús de la Rosa Navarro
Dr Francisco Iriarte Brenner
Director General of Work Relations
Head of the Peruvian Indigenous Institute

***

The Commission's report confirmed the situation and the extent of the work needed. In doing this it reached a watershed for the Asháninka people.

AIDESEP contacted IWGIA in order to submit a project to the Danish government for the titling of indigenous lands in Atalaya, which would serve to support the implementation of the whole programme of reforms that the Peruvian government was recommending and said it was ready to carry out.

With the security of DANIDA support, AIDESEP and the Ministry of Agriculture signed an Agreement, approved via Ministerial Resolution No. 00596-88-AG/DGRAAR of 8th December 1988 to implement a general plan of recognition and territorial titling.

Other chapters of this book deal with the details of the project. It led to a monumental change in the history of the Atalaya region, and set the project apart from other of international cooperation programmes with indigenous people in Peru.

The appearance of invisible citizens

On 5th January 1996, precisely ten years after the incredible pilgrimage of Mr Marinero to Lima, 'El Peruano', the official daily paper of Peru, published a resolution of the National Panel of Electoral Judges, which put an end to a whole long month of doubts. And in spite of the

desperate efforts of the Atalaya estate owners to put political pressure (and economic persuasion) on this Panel, they were unable to do anything about it. The slaves of ten years previous had beaten their former bosses in the local elections fair and square. The Municipality of the Province of Atalaya, one of the largest in Peru, and a good number of the Municipalities of its Districts, had been won by the indigenous movement10. And the same thing had occurred in various Districts and Provinces of Alto Ucayali.

In 1986, local officials had denied the existence of indigenous communities in the region ('no more than six or seven'). The extra-ordinary censuses (Atalaya did not even figure in the 1981 national census) spoke of 8,000 inhabitants, largely mestizos. How was it possible that this insignificant indigenous minority could have won the elections? How was it possible that they had even dared to stand - a humble final list, identified by the number 13 - in the face of the traditional employers' alternatives?

A lot of things had happened over the last decade, the main thing being that the indigenous population had largely liberated itself from the employers and had found dignity in communal life on their ancestral lands once more. The project financed by DANIDA, through

IWGIA, had gained recognition for 71 communities and 168 titles for a total of one million five hundred and thirty seven thousand four hundred and forty one hectares benefitting the Amahuaca, Asháninka, Cacataibo, Cashinahua, Culina, Sharanahua, Shipibo, Yaminahua and Yíne peoples. They had also obtained titles for three Territorial Reserves for the as yet uncontacted peoples of the Mashco-piro, Isconahua and Murunahua, totalling another 1,545,283 hectares. And they had prepared files for four Communal Reserves (El Sira, Inuya-Tahuanía, Yurua and Tamaya-Caco) for a total of 1,318,949 hectares. In total, 4,401,673 hectares, and almost half of all the indigenous lands obtained throughout the whole history of the Peruvian Republic.

Tahuanti, the community which initiated the process by trying to defend its last ten hectares of land ended up with the title to more than six thousand hectares of its traditional territory covered by a dossier of more than 200 pages.

They were ten extremely difficult years. Apart from the tricks of the employers and local authorities, who had not resigned themselves to the 'imposition of justice' by the central government, they also had to cope with a lack of understanding and aggression on the part of Shining Path, many of whose local professionals were children of the bosses who had been stripped of their land through legal actions benefiting the indigenous peoples. But it was already too late and the indigenous peoples had discovered their own strengths. Through their own organisation, OIRA, they had developed a series of peaceful strategies to bring their process of rehabilitation to a successful conclusion. Here the process was peaceful and many poor settlers were helped to relocate outside of the communal lands through fair payment for any improvements they had carried out and support in order to legalize their new pieces of land on uninhabited areas.

In time, OIRA trained the grassroots and, still with Danish support, began a programme of registration and documentation of all the indigenous peoples. The 1993 census states that Atalaya has a population of more than 27,000 inhabitants, a large majority of whom are indigenous. In an area where further colonisation had been prevented during the titling of indigenous lands, the increase in population had to be due to the legal documentation of the indigenous population. The invisible indigenous peoples had, by force, and by their national identity cards, become visible.

When, in the first week of November 1995, former staff of AIDESEP - those who had been there during the most difficult times - were called to give a course on the new and disastrous Land Law, the scene they came across was almost unreal. Atalaya was awash with pre-election posters, all with something in common: all the lists mentioned the indigenous population ('Atalaya and its indigenous communities' cried a poster for an ex-employee of a state body which had affirmed the incapacity of indigenous people to freely organize themselves; 'Put the indigenous first' stated the list of a former slave owner).

But secretly, without posters or declamations, and laughing in the face of all these offers, the indigenous were quietly preparing their own campaign. On the morning of 12th November the Atalaya candidates did not know what to do with their slaughtered cows to win over in extremis the voters. The baskets of bread were untouched and the crates of beer got hot in the sun. The indigenous people, their electoral cards in their hands, came from the areas they had been secretly living in and, in a disciplined manner, were voting for their brothers. And that 12th November went down in history. MIAP was proclaimed the winner of over 8 mestizo seats. The victory was challenged, all possible means were used to avoid the result, but on 5th January 1996 the triumph was confirmed by the National Panel of Electoral Judges.

If the cooperation strategies of the Danish government are aimed at strengthening the potential for democratic influence of the underprivileged populations and their progressive control over their own living conditions, then there is no doubt that the support given to the Ucayali communities has had this result.

But this story has not finished yet. The resources allocated to Atalaya will be extremely limited, and provocations and tricks will doubtless continue. It also has to be recognized that managing a Municipality was not on the agenda of the old Asháninka fighters.

In this next phase, support will be just as important. Good management requires competent and reliable advice. The OIRA-MIAP municipal plans are ambitious and include a total reorganization of the forestry activity of the region, the promotion of productive initiatives on the basis of native resources, the promotion and management of ecological zones, an inventory and organization of the use of regional resources, the strengthening of and opening up of fair trade possibilities on a fair basis, the promotion of indigenous health, the recuperation of culture and national Asháninka dignity within a context of intercultural harmony, the creation of conditions for egalitarian interethnic relations of respect and mutual benefit, a wide diffusion of the knowledge of human rights as well as a broad plan of multidisciplinary training for youth.

Atalaya is an excellent example of how much can be achieved through truly effective international support. Never did cooperation have so much meaning. But in order for this story to have a successful conclusion, this relationship must not be allowed to cool down. Atalaya and its indigenous peoples still expect a great deal from their democratic debut and their recently achieved liberty.

***

Notes

1. Source: Ministry of Agriculture. Quoted in 'Barrantes y Trivelli: Forests and Wood, an economic analysis of the Peruvian case'. IEP 1996.
2. The Inter-Ethnic Association for the Development of the Peruvian Amazon.
3. The traditional tunic of the Asháninka.
4. A selection of these was published in the Peruvian journal Amazonía Indigena Nos. 17 and 18 in 1991. The texts have been altered slightly to make them more comprehensible, but without modifying their substance.
5. Many complaints refer to being hit with the barrel of the paymaster's shotgun.
6. The case of a youth of 16 years old, Grimaldo Pintayo Campos, was submitted to the authorities in Lima after doctors considered it impossible to cure him from the total blindness caused by contusions from a machete wound in the neck.
7. The Mayor's statement is a valuable annex to the IIP report in which he confirms the existence of servile and inhuman conditions in the logging industry of the region.
8. The transcript which follows is part of the extract of the report published in Amazonía Indigena Nos. 17 and 18 in 1991.
9. The British organization 'Anti-Slavery International', the longest standing NGO in Europe dedicated to the protection of human rights, which in 1996 awarded the Atalaya indigenous organization with the 'Anti-Slavery' prize, informed us that this was not the first time that the name of Peru had been linked to problems of this kind. In fact, during the Republican era, Peru had been the country with perhaps the greatest number of complaints regarding the practice of slavery.

   In spite of the fact that San Martín decreed the abolition of slavery in 1821, the importation of slaves from Africa only finally came to an end in 1855, more than 34 years later. Given that agriculture had declined because of the freeing of the black slaves, the estate owners managed to get a law approved on immigration from China in 1849. Under this legislation a sui generis system of slavery was reestablished. The atrocities committed against the Chinese 'coolies' by the coastal estate owners was widely denounced (the Anti-Slavery League was very active in this campaign) and immigration was prohibited in 1854 in the face of an international scandal. Nevertheless, it was reestablished in 1861 and Chinese servitude was maintained until 1890, when 'coolie' work was integrated into the labour system. During 1862 and 1864, Polynesians were imported, for whom the conditions of exploitation were devastating. Peru was once more denounced in international fora, not only for this practice - which was legal in Peru in respect of Polynesians - but because, taking advantage of the law of free importation of Polynesians and given their physical similarity with the indigenous people of the Pacific islands (Easter Island and other neighbouring islands), Peruvian boats were trafficking in Rapa-nui indigenous people. After international protest, They were repatriated carrying illnesses which decimated the populations of these islands (Of these events there is an interesting and well documented story in 'En el país de las colinas de arena' by Fernando de Trazegnies, PUC, 1995).

Once again in 1909, Peru drew attention, following serious complaints in the English newspaper regarding mistreatment of indigenous serfs on the part of the rubber company Arana. The Anti-Slavery League took part in an investigation of the events, headed by Roger Casement who concluded against Arana. In the records of the judgement, Arana admitted holding more than 12,000 indigenous Huitoto, Bora, Andoque and Ocaína within its barracks.

10. The possibility exists in Peru of presenting lists of independent candidates. AIDESEP created a non-partisan list to this end in each electoral process. Its acronym is MIAP - Movimiento Indígena de la Amazonía Peruana - Indigenous Movement of the Peruvian Amazon.

FROM SLAVERY TO DEMOCRACY:
the indigenous process of upper Ucayali and Gran Pajonal

Søren Hvalkof

I. Memmories from the Development Frontier

1. Prologe

The first time I heard of Atalaya was in 1975. As a recent graduate student, I had taken a year off to travel and study the agrarian reform in Peru and as a consequence of a long series of events, I found myself in the heart of indigenous Ashéninka territory in Gran Pajonal. Gran Pajonal is an interfluvial plateau on the eastern side of the Peruvian tropical rain forest. It is one of the last foothills of the Andes stretching into the Amazon region where it rises like a Shangri-la, enclosed between the Pichis-Pachitea, Perené-Tambo and Ucayali rivers (see map p.85). It is populated by a small group of Andean colonists and a majority of Ashéninka Indians who, at that time, were dominated by the colonists who had established themselves as the unquestionable masters of the zone. One day, I was sitting in the earthen kitchen of the local merchant's trading post in the small settlement of Oventeni listening to stories whilst his wife, who took in boarders, was cooking maniok. Her mother was an Piro Indian (Yíne)[1], her father a Spanish rubber patron and she had been brought up in the Franciscan mission's boarding school. She was full of dramatic stories about a life of sacrifice amongst the first settlers in the zone.

Atalaya was mentioned many times, and judging by the tales of the merchant and his wife, this small provincial village was a pearl in the middle of a sea of savagery, a spearhead of civilised culture in the treacherous jungle, populated by totally indomitable Indians. According to the merchant, the small provincial settlement of Atalaya was the centre of the big patrons' business transactions. It was here where they bought their products, here where the patrons had their local businesses, here where the tormented Franciscan mission kept spirits up. Atalaya was the focal point for all river traffic both up and down stream of the Urubamba and its tributaries in southern Peru, as well as being the hub of traffic in both directions on the wild river Tambo and further down along the mighty Ucayali river until you reached the new and expanding city of Pucallpa. Atalaya was also the final destination of larger barges on the Amazon and Ucayali rivers.

According to the merchant's wife, it appeared that the Atalaya patrons were men of different caliber than the Andean colonists and 'wannabe' patrons of Oventeni. They were men of style and culture and many were direct descendants of European entrepreneurs and adventurers who came to the Ucayali to take part in the rubber bonanza at the beginning of this century. The merchant was of the opinion that it would be just my cup of tea to visit these intellectually likeminded people. Furthermore, I would be able to meet a large number of Campa[2] Indians on the haciendas of these patrons, something which apparently would interest me. These patrons would certainly help me and could tell me some things about the life of the savages.

I would really have to visit Atalaya on my way home. They gave me various names of these honourable patrons, together with a description of how to reach their haciendas, down river on the Ucayali. The mistress added that one of the patrons had even transported a piano and velvet furniture to his hacienda. Atalaya and Ucayali had completely different connotations attached than had the upper central forest of Peru, which was colonised by poor Andean peasants. The rain forest of Ucayali was also 'true jungle' - more savage, darker, deeper, higher and unfathomable. Thus, they explained to me, the patrons efforts to civilise the zone were all the more admirable. Ucayali was also haunted with demons not found in other parts, treacherous beings which not even the vanguard of Atalayan civilisation could confront. But the Catholic fathers and sisters did what they could. The señora could recount stories about nude siren seductresses which she herself had seen as a child on the Ucayali river. Atalaya was unquestionably surrounded by myth. Some of the colonists from the Oventeni settlement also mentioned Atalaya, although not with the same aura of romanticism as the merchant's wife, who was a native of Ucayali. For these colonists with an Andean peasant cultural background, Atalaya was not of their world. It was too Amazonian and not Andean enough. But in spite of this, all references to it were reverential. Atalaya was a place where you could make big money and become one of the large patrons, and lumber barons. If only you had your Campas. They told that Atalaya was a place where prisoners and the staff of the Sepa State Penal Colony transacted shady deals and were dangerous to get too close to. The Sepa Penal Colony, which was a day's travel up river on the Urubamba, in the heart of indigenous territory, was a notorious labour camp where long term prisoners and the prison staff exercised a 'self-governing' regime of terror. Sepa was established in 1947 as an amalgamation of a prison and a colonisation project[3]. Sometimes, prisoners managed to escape and the preferred escape route was along the old trails linking Atalaya, Oventeni and Gran Pajonal. Some fugitive prisoners had just been recaptured by the Republican Guard right on the outskirts of Oventeni, having been followed from Atalaya. The inhabitants of Oventeni had sometimes had their previous night's

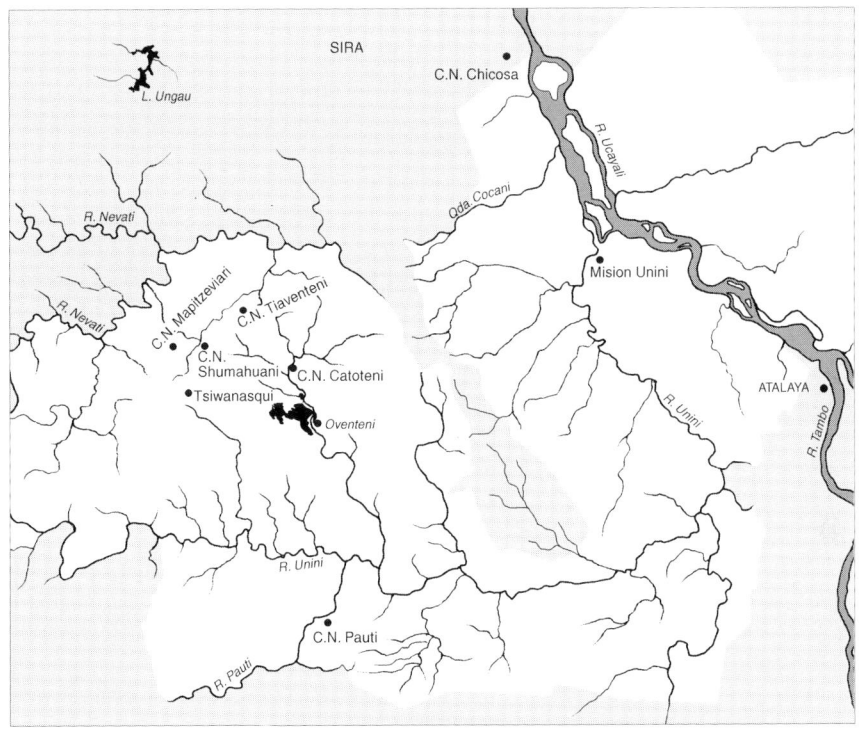

Gran Pajonal and Atalaya

sleep ruined by the scream of the prisoners who were being tortured by the guards. Atalaya and Oventeni were linked, as was the history of Gran Pajonal and that of Ucayali. Oventeni also belonged administratively to the province of Atalaya, as an annexe[4]. Nevertheless, certain ambivalence could be noted amongst the colonists of Oventeni. Although they were impressed by the power of their neighbouring patrons, they did not feel sure about their control and although they were in constant contact with Atalaya, the colonists of Oventeni at that time had managed to transfer the political and public administration of Gran Pajonal to the province of Satipo where their friends and relatives lived, where there was a clear cultural identification and where, due to these two factors, they could manipulate the regional power structure. In Atalaya, power was not directly accessible by "highlanders"of the Andes.

This contradiction between the true historical relationship of Gran Pajonal and Atalaya and the cultural roots of the inhabitants of Oventeni in Andean peasant culture subsequently came to play a determining role in the political organisation of the indigenous population.

During my first, relatively short, stay in Gran Pajonal[5] more stories about the Atalaya zone gradually emerged which unfortunately made the mythical descriptions of the merchant's wife lose some of their force. At first, they were limited to insinuations and vague comments, but they soon became complex explanations which all agreed that not all of the Atalaya patrons were God's best children and that several of them had been heavily involved in the so-called "correrías", in which some of the Oventeni colonists had also participated. "Correrías" are rapid slave raids which became institutionalised during the rubber boom around the turn of the century, to obtain labourers for the rubber extraction. A patron would give a small group of slave hunters Winchester rifles, which were in great demand, in return for which Ashéninka settlements were attacked and all individuals potentially capable of working taken captive, that is, preferably children and young women, who were taken to the patron as his personal property. Adult men were more difficult to control and thus they were preferably killed, to avoid witnesses and possible reprisals. These parties frequently consisted of Indians, who had long been subjugated by the patron through debt bondage. The Ashéninka, Yíne and Conibo were all active in these correrías. But colonists also participated as leaders of raiding parties. Although everyone assured us that these occurrences were fortunately a thing of the past, the correrías had apparently been taking place up to the 1960s. The favourite focus of the Atalaya patrons' correrías had been the isolated Ashéninka settlements in the relatively inaccessible transitional zone between Gran Pajonal and Ucayali. Without doubt, I was going to find many of the Indians from Gran Pajonal on these haciendas, as the merchant had explained to me.

Nevertheless, I did not spend all of my time during this preliminary field work listening to horrible fables and idle gossip in Oventeni. I spent most of it with a couple of Ashéninka families who were preparing their swiddens and planting their new annual crops. It was the end of the dry summer season when hunting is scarce and when only small fish can be caught in the few streams that have not completely dried up. As mentioned, Gran Pajonal is an interfluvial zone, which lacks navigable rivers, only drained by rapid white-water rivers. The menu at this time of year was practically vegetarian, occasionally supplemented by small animals such as insects, snails, fry and other similar "animalitos". For this reason they also talked a lot about Ucayali, a true fishing paradise. The preferred contacts of the Ashéninka of Gran Pajonal, outside of their territory, are their Ashéninka relatives of the Upper Ucayali. The two areas are linked by an old network of trails and the inhabitants of the Pajonal love to go on family fishing trips to the Ucayali. It only takes an Ashéninka a couple of days to get there and they will happily spend a month down stream from Atalaya, where they fish, eat and trade with their partners. Ucayali is the door to the outside world. It is also here where the most adventurous can find a patron to work for - if they feel like it. It is quite common for young Ashéninka from Gran Pajonal to contract work as lumber-jacks for the patrons. It is very hard work which is dreadfully paid. But it gives them the opportunity of getting around a little in the lower Amazon region. My Ashéninka hosts also told me about the correrías and how often the Ucayali slave hunters had attacked the settlements of Gran Pajonal. Indigenous persons who were contracted to hunt slaves were known as Ovayeri[6] - which they translated into Spanish as "criminals". And they knew many ex-criminals. They almost always entered the zone by the Unini river, a river of rapid currents whose source lies in the western Gran Pajonal and which flows into the Ucayali river just below Atalaya. Curiously the term "criminal" was not used for the patrons who sponsored them, nor for those who appropriated the abducted children. At that time, in indigenous consciousness, the patrons, by definition, belonged to another category of human beings relating to a completely different context, distanced from common moral concepts of just and unjust. The patrons were justice, they embodied justice, they held power and defined meaning and opinion. The slave hunters were criminals because they killed, not because they took slaves - the patrons were just patrons. This was how things were back in 1975. Twenty years later the term Ovayeri was to take on a completely different significance.

There is no doubt that Atalaya and the Upper Ucayali took on an important role in the consciousness of the inhabitants of Gran Pajonal. All reference to Atalaya was dramatic, ambivalent, and with an underlying tone of cruelty. Stories often appeared unreal, as if they belonged to a far-off time. Atalaya seemed an anachronistic island in history. In any case, my curiosity was awakened and so I decided to visit the region once more, going via Atalaya and down stream by the Ucayali with whatever river transport there was.

The journey by plane in a one engine Cessna from Oventeni to Atalaya took 17 minutes. In comparison with Oventeni, which was only the size of fifty or so wooden houses with palm leaf rooves, a grass landing strip and a yellow tiled church with its corresponding school and missionary building, Atalaya was a town. Not a big town, but a town nevertheless, with streets, a plaza with its obligatory monument, a couple of hotels, an active Franciscan mission, a police station, a legal office, representatives of different authorities, businesses, shops, and various restaurants and bars. Atalaya, (which means the view or the hillock), lies on a corner where the Tambo and Urubamba rivers meet, and where the Ucayali river begin. (see map p.85). The setting is beautiful, a fact which the merchant's wife in Oventeni had frequently noted. We arrived in Atalaya in the afternoon and went straight to the hotel we had been recommended, where the owner received us with the expression, "Welcome to the Republic of Atalaya!". It would later be seen that there was much more truth in this expression than was immediately apparent. Colonist society in Atalaya truly considered itself to be above the national laws and justice. They followed their own rules and laws[7].

Nevertheless, it struck me that on the way from the airport to the plaza, where the hotel was situated, we saw not one indigenous person. Although the facial features and appearance of the inhabitants of Atalaya suggested a diverse range of backgrounds, I saw no-one who I could state with certainty was an Ashéninka. In Oventeni there were always Ashéninka, dressed in their traditional "cushma" - a cotton tunic which they wear down to their ankles - with different feather decorations, bow and arrows hanging from the shoulder, baskets and beautifully painted with annatto dye and black pencil lines on the face. During this stay in Atalaya I saw only one person dressed in a cushma, and he was a skinny and pitiful lad of 13 or 14 years of age who was wearing an old and frayed cushma which looked more like a sack. He was standing waiting on the plaza, where he was picked-up by his patron. He was the only one. The answer to my questions as to why there were no Indians to be seen in Atalaya was that they were working on the haciendas of their patrons and when they occasionally came to the town they generally stayed on the beach near to their canoes (Cf. Veber 1992, 1996, on the significance of the cushma in forming identity.)

The hotel owner, who was of Brazilian origin, tried to convince me to stay in Atalaya, "because we need new European settlers" to ensure modern progress. He offered to find me free land and indigenous labourers, provided I stayed. I politely turned down this proposal and after several days waiting I continued my journey down stream in a minor river launch whose skipper entertained me for a week with most incredible stories. Thus the first chapter of my odyssey ended in the optimistic reality of Amazonian lands and I returned home to a much colder north European reality.

The Ashéninka of Gran Pajonal were undoubtedly extremely pressurised and exploited by the colonists of Oventeni, but they had, nevertheless, their own identity and generally did what they wanted, their language was thriving, their subsistence economy functioned and they were not behaving like the remains of a dying culture, or as social relics condemned to disappear in the grind mill of history. Although other Campa groups from other zones had been overwhelmed by colonisation, Gran Pajonal and the Upper Ucayali were still populated in the majority by indigenous people who, in spite of the patrons' terror, maintained an identity, a culture and a territory. The condition

Asháninka family from the begining of this century

Ferdinand Stahl baptizes Asháninka near Río Perené (ca. 1928)

for them to be able to continue this other world in one way or another was, however, that they have a space to do it in. That they are able to maintain, control and reproduce a territory - both physical and symbolic. And this guarantee did not exist in 1975[8]. The Ashéninka families I stayed with were extremely clear about the problem. Both Sebastián and his son Juancito, in Catoteni, had expressed their concern regarding the constant expansion of the colonists, and Ikaniteri, who I had the opportunity of meeting whilst bartering a shot gun, had asked me to stay and teach and help them to organise with the aim of obtaining land rights. He was later to become one of the biggest shamans of the area, and he was one of the first headmen to obtain a land title for his local group. His brother, who was a headman in Ucayali, did the same. Ikaniteri was one of the focal points of the traditional Ashéninka exchange network, the so-called Ayompari system (cf. Bodley 1973, Schäfer 1988). He obtained a great deal of information in this way, and he was concerned with what he heard. He explained to me that they had an old missionary school with furniture and a blackboard, but they had no teacher. It was in Tiaventeni, a part of Gran Pajonal where the Adventist mission had had a missionary station which had now moved to Pauti, situated more centrally on one of the main trails. The old school was no longer in use. I explained that I was not a Seventh Day Adventist nor a missionary, but neither was he and he did not really care as long as I could teach and help him and his group to organise. When I asked him how he imagined I would live if I agreed to this, he rapidly replied, "We have enormous quantities of maniok". Unfortunately, I was forced to turn down this interesting offer but I promised him, Sebastián and Juancito that I would do what I could to find a solution and to return when something occurred to me.

Their situation was worrying. They had almost everything to lose and they were far distant from the political decision making processes. In 1975, there was still no real indigenous movement in Peru. Some of the Marxist-oriented peasant unions, operating closer towards the Andes, certainly had Asháninka members, but in no way did they consider the special needs of the indigenous peoples in terms of language, culture and territory. Such issues were referred to the section in charge of folkloric events for Sunday bazaars and other holiday festivals. That a political organisation of indigenous people could base itself on a platform of identity and culture was unthinkable and dismissed as romantic or directly as a reactionary thought. Integration, assimilation, economic progress, development and modernity were on the agenda then. A way of resolving the problem of the expanding colonist society had to be found. A guarantee of indigenous lands, be it through titles or in whatever form, seemed an obvious precondition which had to be achieved. The problem was to device and implement a viable strategy by which to achieve this, but time was not ripe yet.

2. The Birth of the Indigenous Movements

But changes were under way. The concept of indigenous peoples and their rights was slowly finding its way onto the political agendas. Around 1968, committed anthropologists and other academics, motivated by empirical experiences, set up the first organisations in support of the rights of indigenous peoples. This included, amongst others, IWGIA, which has its offices in Copenhagen; Survival International in London and Cultural Survival in Boston. Many more were to emerge in the following years. In South America, the first indigenous organisation of the Amazon was born at the same time, as an institution independent of the State and of existing political organisations. Thus in 1964, the 'Federación de los Centros Shuar en el Oriente de Ecuador' was established as an answer to the growing pressures from colonisation (Cf., Salazar 1977 for a detailed description). The initiative originally arose amongst the Salesian Catholic missionaries who, amongst other things, began a system of bilingual intercultural schooling by radio (Shuar, Spanish) - a revolutionary approach at the time. The Shuar gradually took full control of the organisation, which in the following decade was an exemplary model[9]. Over the next decade, many new indigenous organisations emerged. But also the international arena for human rights and development, was opening its eyes to the particular problems of indigenous peoples. The World Council of Churches[10], in cooperation with the anthropology department of the University of Bern (Switzerland), sponsored the first international symposium on indigenous rights and problems in South America[11]. The symposium was held in Barbados in January 1971, with the participation of anthropologists from many South American countries, the United States of America and Europe. It gave birth to a joint resolution, the so called "Barbados Declaration" ("For the liberation of Indians") (Doc. 1:1971) which was one of the first Latin American initiatives for an international indigenous policy. The principal theme of the declaration was "accountablitity." It specified the right of indigenous peoples to self-determination and self-management and specified the responsibilities, duties and rights which could be imposed on the four main players in the process: the State, the religious missions, anthropology as a discipline and the indigenous peoples themselves. The World Council of Churches then published a compilation of the country studies which had been presented to the symposium (Dostal 1972). The declaration was the first paper that IWGIA published in its documentation series, which today consists of more than 120 publications. Other organisations supporting indigenous peoples also published case studies and newsletters and over the next decade a wealth of detailed documentation became available.

The situation of the Asháninka and Ashéninka groups had also been described, and warning lights turned on. The Peruvian anthropologist, Stefano Varese, published his excellent work "La Sal de los Cerros" (The Salt of the Mountains) in 1968 (1973), which dealt with the history, ethnography, mythology and current situation of the Campa groups. Varese, who as a student in the beginning of the 1960s had carried out field work in Gran Pajonal based in Oventeni, was one of the participants at the Barbados seminar and he continued writing more general articles on ethno-political issues (e.g. Varese 1982). He visited IWGIA at the beginning of the 1970s, where he gave a seminar at the University of Copenhagen. He spoke about the current situation of the indigenous groups of the Peruvian Amazon. In 1972, IWGIA published his document "The Forest Indians in the Present Situation of Peru". However, it did not deal explicitly with the feudal system in the province of Atalaya.

This was, however, done by another committed anthropologist, the American John H. Bodley. He had similarly carried out field studies amongst Ashéninka groups in the regions of Gran Pajonal, Upper Ucayali and Pichis. His 1970 doctoral dissertation 'Campa Socio-Economic Adaptation' among other issues documented and analysed the relations between the patrons and the indigenous population and, in 1972, IWGIA published its first work explicitly on the situation of the Ashéninka: "Tribal Survival in the Amazon: the Campa Case), which is an extract from his thesis. This draws attention to the generalised expansion of slave raiding up until the 1940s and the death, destruction and disaster which these activities inflicted on the Indians of Ucayali and Gran Pajonal. However, he was not aware of how serious and contemporary the situation in Atalaya was.

But in spite of the fact that an awareness was beginning to rise around indigenous people's problems in wider intellectual circles, it was still decades before the international development sphere, public administration and political decision makers recognised the relevance of the issue. Although the "savages" in general had become fashionable in Europe in the Utopian and aesthetic literature of the 1970s and '80s, it was largely as one element in a completely eurocentric discourse - a narcissistic reflection of the philosophical schism and identity crisis which was unfolding in the western world as a result of the ongoing collapse of the modernist ideals and rationality. It was not an expression of political solidarity with the indigenous people's struggle for a reasonable standard of living and self-determination. Nor in anthropology in general did there exist a greater understanding of political responsibility with regard to the indigenous peoples and, in this context, advocacy was generally relegated to the category of romantic and unscientific activism (Cf. Hastrup and Elsass 1990). Meanwhile, the indigenous peoples were organising, supported in the process by active and committed students and intellectuals, both from developing countries and from Europe and the USA. Local, regional and national organisations emerged on all sides and these new social movements gradually managed to gain political importance within national development processes. In Peru, the first regional indigenous organisations were established a the end of the 1970s, and in 1980 their national umbrella organisation, AIDESEP was set up.

10 years after in 1985 I returned once more to Gran Pajonal to carry out a two and a half year research project[12].

II. The first stage - the process in Gran Pajonal

1. Historical cycles

a. The colonial period
Pajonal - the great grassland - is so called because of the many open areas of grass, both large and small, which are scattered throughout the region. In reality, natural pasture makes up less than 4% of the plateau which defines the zone (Denevan and Chrostowski 1970, Scott 1979, Hvalkof 1985, Hvalkof and Veber 1998), and the name is, to a large extent, a metaphor for the development dream which the Franciscan missionaries who colonised the zone for the first time in the 1730s had: the establishment of an enormous cattle raising zone under the management of the mission, supported by appropriate Spanish colonisation and a pacified, obedient and Christian indigenous population providing a cheap and loyal work force. (Ortiz 1961:50)[13]. At the same time, the zone would operate as the logistical link between the Franciscan colonisation in the eastern Andean region and the lower part of the Amazon via the Ucayali river. In general it caused great difficulties to colonise the enormous tropical rain forests of the eastern foothills of the Amazonian Andes. The indigenous peoples of the zone, had rebelled a few years after the establishment of the first mission in the Selva Central in 1635 and had totally destroyed the mission. In an endless spiral of colonising attempts, growing reprisals and more and larger rebellions, it went from confrontation to confrontation, whilst the number of Franciscan martyrs grew steadily. (Amich 1988, Izaguirre 1924, Ortiz 1961, Santos 1987). Shortly before the colonisation of Gran Pajonal reached its zenith in 1738 with the establishment of 10

cattle ranches, blacksmiths and missions scattered throughout the zone, the mission had carried out a massive punitive expedition coordinated on two fronts in the Andean zones neighbouring Gran Pajonal, with the support of two contingents of Spanish troops from the Viceroy in Lima. They had executed four popular local Asháninka leaders and erected their heads and hands on posts. The Franciscans were thus exalted by the fact that they had received an unexpected positive reception in Gran Pajonal. However the positive attitude was due more to the fact that the missionaries had bought the loyalty of the local headmen with metal tools and liquor and thus strengthened their position and prestige in the local trading network. (Hvalkof and Veber 1998). But the mission's did not have an endless supply of resources and rumours regarding the executions caused suspicion. The unexpected peace in Gran Pajonal was no more than a vain illusion. The settling of old scores with the Spanish colonial power and the Franciscan mission began right in Gran Pajonal[14] in 1742, where the Indians held a mass meeting attended by more than a thousand Ashéninka and representatives from other indigenous groups to declare that the missionaries were not wanted and to promise armed resistance against the oppression of the Spanish viceroyalty (Amich 1988: 166-172). When the viceroyalty, months later, finally intervened militarily in Gran Pajonal with 70 soldiers and 20 indigenous archers, they found only a small arms deposit which they captured after a hard fight with the local Ashéninka "cacique", Mateo Santobangori, who was killed along with 12 of his defence guard. According to the Franciscan reports, the Spanish army suffered no losses, but many were wounded. This report regarding losses is, however, not very certain and is, of course, stained with the desperation of the Franciscans (Ortiz 1961:56). But the leadership of the rebellion and the main militia could not be found. They had moved to the strategically more central zone of the valley of the upper Perené, at the door to the Andes. There they established general headquarters in the former Metraro mission which included both Asháninka and Yanesha. The person behind this global expansion of indigenous resistance was Juan Santos, with the opulent byname of "Atahualpa Apu Inka", a charismatic character who appeared on the scene by chance and who, for the next 11 years, together with a group of chiefs from the zone, coordinated a united resistance against the Spanish and organised a permanent indigenous militia which was to reestablish full indigenous control over the whole area of the Peruvian Selva Central (cf., Castro Arenas 1973, Lehnertz 1972, Metraux 1942, Ortiz 1961, Santos Granero 1987, 1992; Zazar 1989, Varese 1973). The rebellion was followed by other large uprisings in the neighbouring riverine zones and the colonial power never again managed to reestablish itself.

b. State expansion and modernisation

More than 100 years passed before colonisation and infrastructural development were reintroduced, this time by the new Peruvian State, which had been through a long and tumultuous war of independence and whose economy was in a state of latent disorder. Meanwhile, a new extractivist economy had been developed in the forest region: rubber extraction and slave trade by the Ucayali patrons. In Gran Pajonal, slave raids and the transportation of slaves between the great river systems to the east and through the Andean forest regions heralded a period of particularly great disintegration which separated families, forced people from their homes, destroyed the social organisation and traditional system of alliances. At the same time violent measles epidemics haunted, which aggravated the situation. At around the turn of the century a number of different expeditions were carried out across Gran Pajonal, sponsored by the State in order to study the possibilities of reintroducing colonisation, again under the auspices of the Franciscans (Sala 1887). The objective was the same as that of 150 years previous: the development of a large scale cattle raising zone, the pacification of the Ashéninka, colonisation and European investment and now also the construction of a rail link from Chanchamayo across Gran Pajonal as far as Ucayali and the great river systems. But the dream of technological progress on the great grasslands was still far from realisation, and most of the plans were abandoned due to incalculable logistical problems.

The State was luckier with the reconquest of the neighbouring zones towards the Andes. New plans for colonist settlements, agriculture, cattle raising and infrastructure were made, all of them based on the erroneous idea that the zone held tremendous economic potential and that the indigenous population would provide the necessary labour - a fantasy which seems to have continued up to this day. As part of a deal for settling a major national debt with British creditors following a Peruvian State bankruptcy, the Peruvian government in 1891 handed over a concession area of some 2,000,000 hectares to the British-owned Peruvian Corporation, in the Central Peruvian jungle (Selva Central). The area was targeted for agriculture, extraction and other economic developments with all the native inhabitants as indentured labour. Although the corporation in actual fact "only" managed to utilise some 500,000 hectares, it established large plantations of coffee and other export crops, and was notorious for its inhumane working conditions, in closed colonies resembling concentration camps[15]. The Asháninka population was now under pressure from two sides. From the direction of the Andes, the agricultural frontier was advancing rapidly and from the direction of Ucayali, the extractivist economy was expanding, with a growing need for indigenous indentured labour.

As recently as 1935, the Franciscan mission reestablished the first missionary posts on the grasslands of Gran Pajonal. Only one of these survived: the small Oventeni colony. The main reason for this was the 1,600 metre long landing strip which was subsequently built and which was regularly used by the Peruvian army to maintain open the supply lines for colonisation and so that they could bring in troops if the Ashéninka rebelled. There were a number of sporadic attempts to get rid of the intruding settlers, but all met with a crudely violent response. At this time the Ashéninka population was still extremely small in numbers and divided: a consequence of the atrocities of the rubber period.

The colonisation of the zone turned out to be quite difficult. It was almost impossible to find interested settlers, and so the mission devoted itself to attracting poor indigenous peasants from the Andes to Oventeni, with contracts which put them in a position of servitude towards the church and tied to the zone for many years. There were constant conflicts in the colonisation; the Ashéninka were hostile and many contracted settlers simply fled. Cattle farming was not the great success that had been hoped for and coffee production had to be expanded as an alternative. But in 1950, this panorama changed radically. Investors from Lima, with connections with the mission, established a large cattle ranch in the interior of Gran Pajonal: Florestal Ganadera S.A. The extensive natural pastures should now be rationally used and the company built an impressive infrastructure: a hacienda with houses for the workers, technicians and foremen, veterinary facilities, a sawmill, wooden fences etc. They carried out technical studies, aerial photographic surveys and land measurements. They bought high quality cattle and breeding stock, as well as creating a good head of horses, mules and donkeys. They employed a veterinarian, a doctor and other technical specialists according to need. Workers were contracted in Lima and in the highland under good conditions, and very soon there was no problem in gaining the necessary work force. Optimism was great and colonisation flourished. The new economic expansion also brought about a spontaneous colonisation by enterprising highlanders.

Relations with the Ashéninka were still murky, and there was great resentment amongst the indigenous population regarding the fact that the white "wiracocha" - along with their cattle - were establishing themselves all over just like that. The cattle caused a great deal of damage to the crops and settlements and there were constant conflicts. There were pockets of conspiracy but the estate was well armed with powerful military rifles and the foreman took advantage of the existing rivalries and divisions between local headmen, some of whom were employed by the company. Furthermore, loyalty was secured through the distribution of western medicine and medical aid. Unfortunately, the indigenous population was once more suffering from violent measles epidemics which the many immigrants and migrant workers had brought in to the area from outside. Ex-estate workers told me that many of the sick Ashéninka sought refuge on the hacienda in the hope of being cured, but that they "died like flies". People were buried every day, not mentioning the many deaths outside of the hacienda. Many fled to neighbouring zones or went deep into the rugged forest zones towards the Sira mountains to the north of Gran Pajonal, which are practically unpopulated. The depopulation was catastrophic and yet the hacienda continued to operate unperturbed. But in spite of the capital, the specialists and the work force, it was not such an economic success. Significant administrative problems, low profitability, logistic problems, excess investment, cattle sickness and the fact that the natural pastures had a relatively low nutritional value; all these factors pointed to a new fiasco. The death sentence arrived in the winter of 1965/66 when the legendary guerrilla leader, Guillermo Lobatón, of the MIR (Movimiento Izquierda Revolucionario), withdrew his forces back across Gran Pajonal and, in the absence of the administrator of the hacienda (who they threatened with death) the last of the valuable breeding bulls were slaughtered. The guerrillas were defeated in Mapitzeviari, in Gran Pajonal, by American trained counter-insurgency forces "the Rangers", who were transported to Oventeni by plane[16] (cf. Brown and Fernández 1991:164-188)For the next three years the army set up a base in Oventeni, where the soldiers spent most of their time drinking, bothering the colonists in general and abusing the women in particular[17]. In spite of the guerrillas' military defeat and annihilation, in one way their mere presence partly achieved their objective. The mission's boarding school, which had had a particularly negative effect on Ashéninka society by forcing parents to hand over their children, was closed for security reasons and all the monks were evacuated. The cattle venture was finally abandoned in 1968 and the Indians began returning to their former territories. The dream of the formidable development on the great grasslands was frustrated once more.

c. Development and globalization

The years following 1968 were generally characterised by a global breakdown in the system of values established by the western world and a growing internationalisation of the economy and politics. Gran Pajonal was no exception. The evangelist missionaries of the North American Summer Institute of Linguistics (SIL) were permanently established and began to systematically consolidate a bilingual school system as part of their missionary strategy. Potential teachers/bible translators were recruited amongst the Ashéninka youth and sent on courses to receive higher education at the missionary organisation's

Gran Pajonal

Oventeni

base. The missionaries also began to immunise the indigenous population, which was undoubtedly one of the reasons why the population began to increase once more. One of the greatest problems which the Christian missionaries always had in the recruitment of converts amongst the Ashéninka was their dispersed settlements, their great mobility and the absence of permanent and formal administrative structures. Thus the old mission strategy of concentration has always been central although the ways of achieving this have changed over time. The evangelists tried to set up schools and identifying local headmen who were in favour of the idea, hoping that the people would then gather around these new "shared" centres. To ensure the survival of the schools and the centre image, landing strips were established where the small planes of the mission could land. They thus tried to solve the classical problem of logistics and ensure supervision and follow up to the work of the missionary schools and also the provision of health services and a limited air ambulance service. The SIL strategy of being modern medicine men and people of resources strengthened the prestige of the local headmen and the dependency on the mission's services, a strategy which structurally resembled that which had been used by the Franciscans during the first attempts at colonisation in the 1730s (cf., Hvalkof and Aaby 1981).

This development happened to coincide with the Peruvian agrarian reform which the left-liberal President, General Velasco Alvarado, had been implementing since his military coup of 1968. Under the programme of reforms, special legislation was formulated for the indigenous communities of the Amazon, called "native communities". According to this indigenous settlements could be registered as Comunidades Nativas, which would grant them certain special rights, one of which was the possibility of obtaining collective property rights to their land[18]. This model was a direct copy of the legislation for Andean peasant communities, which have a completely different corporate structure. They live in villages and have a production system which is essentially different. Thus the new legislation was badly adapted to the reality of Amazonian indigenous society. However it was still of great importance. The Ashéninka groups and their neighbours in particular quickly reinterpreted the law so that it was in line with their territorial concept, so that a community did not mean a village but an area of land with its corresponding dispersed population. Thus a coinciding cross-field suddenly appeared between the organisational focalising of the missions and the government's rural legislation, which opened up new possibilities for the Ashéninka, and it was not long before they took advantage of this momentum. After the collapse of the cattle project, most of the colonists found themselves in limbo. Some of the former hacienda workers left Oventeni once again, whilst others stayed on to work as individual producers. Most devoted themselves to coffee production for a time, which at one point gave reasonable prices and was a product with transportation advantages in comparison to beef. The Ashéninka took care of most of the production of the community; their labour was ensured through debt bondage and patron-peon relationships. The model was an adaptation of the feudal structures of accumulation to which the same settlers had been subjected in the Andes. The settlers looked upon the organisational initiatives of the Protestant mission with increasing mistrust, although they could not have imagined what was lying in wait for them. Their main interest was to ensure that the tie to the indigenous work force was not broken through different forms of settlement and independent production, and so they sharpened the ideological rhetoric in Oventeni whilst the Ashéninka, as skilled pragmatists, took no definite position one way or the other and still avoided open conflict. It should also be noted that the settlers were an important source of arms, munitions, tools, useful and decorative articles and other things that the Ashéninka had no other means of obtaining. Thus they often looked for a patron-peon relationship although the human and labour costs of achieving this were extremely high.

But in the zones around Gran Pajonal, other development were under way. At the beginning of the 1970s, the State carried out large distributions of land and built a new road network with links to Lima, so that the colonisation of the zone could be widened and consolidated. More adventurous individuals also went as far as Oventeni and Atalaya to see if it was possible to gain something. The great boost arrived with the return of civil government to Peru in 1978, which re-opened the access to international development projects, State loans and credits for development, which had been frozen during the military regime. The new President elect, Fernando Belaúnde Terry, was an old acquaintance, the same president who had been brought down by the military coup 12 years previously. Belaúnde was an architect, he had always been absorbed by the myth of the enormous agricultural potential of the Amazon and he was convinced that the achievement of large scale and planned colonisation would liberate its potential, which would be able to save the economy of the country[19]. Ambitious road construction was carried out in the Amazonian region, along with the so-called Special Projects for integrated development, including the widening of credit possibilities to smaller cattle farmers, all financed and supervised by the international development banks and similar institutions[20]. The road never reached Gran Pajonal, although there was constant pressure from the settlers for it to do so. But credit did reach there, along with a wider market and the illusion that large-scale progress was underway. As the price of coffee at this time was at an all-

time low, cattle farming was the only known alternative and something new was tried: planting different fodder grasses on land cleared in the forest. This coincided with new programmes of credit to small cattle farmers, which the Peruvian government indiscriminately channelled through its extension offices of the agrarian development bank.

This was a great success and from 1980 on the forest was cleared and pasture was planted and cattle were produced like never before, all done by Ashéninka labour, which was the only feasible method by which the colonists could invest. The brutal exploitation of the indigenous work force reached new limits and the expansion of cattle farming created an enormous increase in the conflicts between the colonists and the Ashéninka regarding the question of land ownership. Indians who did not fulfil their "work contracts" with the colonists were imprisoned and punished physically, whipped with a dried bull's penis, the so called "chicote", in the small gaol of Oventeni. This was an institutionalised and formal ritual which took place every Sunday. The colonist authorities, who were appointed by the colonists themselves, regularly formed so called commissions to look for indebted workers who had fled, in order to take them to Oventeni for punishment. Mistreatment and torture were commonplace (Hvalkof 1986, Schäfer 1988) and in 1984 a whole family with children, 14 in total, committed collective suicide by drinking poison, because of the torture and humiliation to which two of the men were subjected during a week of imprisonment in the Oventeni lock-up. Nobody was ever found responsible for such atrocities, in spite of publication, protests and denunciations to the highest magistrates.

3. Organisation and land titling

Naturally, the Ashéninka population was not the passive spectator of its own destruction. They kept abreast of developments and little by little they began to organise politically and, as far as possible, used the Protestant mission as a lever. It should be emphasised in this respect that the Catholic church of Oventeni, for obvious historical reasons, identified fully with colonist society and its interests, and was actively opposed to any form of indigenous organisation, and challenged the bilingual education promoted by the North American Protestant mission. Thus, the indigenous alliance with the SIL had a clear political motivation and interest and cannot be conceived as a spiritual phenomenon, although the missionaries prefer to explain it as such.

Young leaders had begun to stand out amongst the Ashéninka and they tried to put in place an organisational process. New missionaries, who thought speedy action was necessary, had arrived. The SIL and the new indigenous dirigentes, who were all teachers in the SIL's bilingual schools, had held a sort of annual assembly from the 1970s onwards, in Chiquitavo where the SIL had a house, radio and landing strip. Obviously the assembly mostly focussed on schools, teaching and recruitment of teachers. Special guests and authorities from Peruvian national society were also invited to Gran Pajonal to participate and getting to know the place, its problems and the work of the SIL. Apart from the direct motivation of helping to build an organisation, the long term expectation of the mission was at some stage that the indigenous organization would become an evangelical ecclesiastical society as well as having a political role, perhaps with the hope of avoiding a leftist oriented politicisation[21]. But developments were taking another direction. Due to an increase in the intensity of the underlying conflict, the meetings took on an ever more political character and this politicisation also included the SIL missionaries. The emerging indigenous dirigentes were now insisting that the SIL began demarcation of indigenous territories in order to curb colonist expansion. With the help of a Protestant humanitarian aid organisation, funding was obtained to demarcate and measure the first four native communities which were formed in Gran Pajonal[22]. In a lightning action, the SIL mission rushed in a team of surveyors from the Ministry of Agriculture in Pucallpa, which carried out the demarcation relatively rapidly. The technical quality of the work was questionable, but a first step had been taken in the reconquest of lost territories. The settlers naturally considered this totally absurd and accused the male missionaries of the SIL of subversive activity, of being against development and of arousing the innocent Indians to rebel against the advocates of civilisation, the Oventeni colonists. One interesting detail is that anonymous colonists, in an article in a local newspaper from the neighbouring colonist town of Satipo, accused the SIL missionary of having "anti-civilisationary" intentions, writing that he wore a cushma and painted his fast with red annatto dye (Colono Equis 1985). (It must be noted in parentheses that I believe I have never seen him in anything but a recently washed tee shirt and shorts, always clean shaven and without a trace of makeup!)

These first four communities which were demarcated in Gran Pajonal in 1984 covered a large part of the concession area of the old cattle farming estate and thus it was naturally of positive symbolic value that it was precisely these areas of grassland which were now returning into indigenous hands and, what was more, as legalised collective private property with titles. But the demarcation of the four zones did not halt the overall expansion of the settlers' cattle economy. On the contrary, it infuriated the colonists who replied with an escalation of repression and an acceleration of forest clearing and establishment of new areas of pasture. Conflicts with the indigenous population increased alarmingly. The SIL had exhausted its political and economic possibilities for

continuing the demarcation process and a truly representative indigenous organisation was still in the making in Gran Pajonal. AIDESEP and other national indigenous movements which were consolidating at this time already had enough to do in other better known and more accessible areas of the Amazon.

At this time I returned to Gran Pajonal to carry out the previously mentioned research project. It was 1985[23], and I immediately found myself involved in the serious situation. In the first months following my return an overall demographic and economic survey was carried out, in which I visited and interviewed almost a third of the population of Gran Pajonal. It soon became clear that official statistics for the zone were completely incorrect and that all the information issued by the public administration was produced by the colonists themselves and approved by the public hierarchy which, at least at a regional level, was characterised by a coincidence of ideology and interests between the colonists and the administrators (cf., Hvalkof 1990). Thus both the content and the choice of information was extensively manipulated. As the Ashéninka began to understand what was meant by being a community, more and more local groups began to form communities and to request their demarcation, especially as the conflict escalated. The situation was discussed with the indigenous dirigentes of Gran Pajonal and they decided to try to obtain instant demarcation and legalisation of as many communities as possible, since indigenous control of the territory seemed to be the only immediate solution.

The settlers, who also saw the signs, naturally defended their economic interests as cattle raisers and requested that all development initiatives which involved the public administration should be under the responsibility of the province of Satipo, although most of Gran Pajonal belonged to the province of Atalaya in Ucayali. The aim of this administrative trick was to maintain control over the process and information, since the Satipo administration, as previously mentioned, was the essence of colonist culture and had the same identifying background as the Oventeni colonists as well as vested interests in the zone. Thus they tried to find a way of pushing such regional interests to one side. It was decided to try to involve the Special Projects themselves, which had been part of the cause of the problem. The reasons were the following: they were not connected with local or regional interests but were dependent upon the Ministry of the President; their staff was made up of officials with an acceptable technical training who were largely from Lima and had no economic interests in the region; they made the decisions with regard to questions relating to agrarian development plans; they had their own procedures, budgets and technical teams and they were funded and supervised by international development agencies which could supposedly intervene.

All resources and networks were mobilised. We handed in demographic, spatial, ecological, historical and ethnographic data, and lobbying work in the administration of the "special projects" was begun. The Ashéninka dirigentes travelled on foot or with borrowed money to the provincial capital and to Lima to follow up the case. A special report was drawn up on the situation, with descriptions, analysis and recommendations and it was immediately sent to the World Bank in Washington D.C. (Hvalkof 1986a). It blamed the World Bank, which was funding colonisation projects in the immediate border zones (PEPP Satipo-Chanchamayo Programme), for the potential ecological and social catastrophe which was underway, together with a proposal as to how to change the situation through the demarcation and allocation of property rights to the Ashéninka[24]. To the great surprise of all, the World Bank reacted rapidly and positively. Based on the report, they sent an external consultant to look into the situation and he confirmed its analysis and recommended the demarcation of the native communities of Gran Pajonal as a possible solution. The PEPP was then pressurised to take responsibility and carry out the demarcation as quickly as possible.

Out of this process emerged a real and independent indigenous organisation, OAGP[25], which duly established itself with leadership posts, statutes, a general assembly and rubber stamps. After violent conflicts and complex intrigues between colonist society and its allies in the regional administration on the one hand and the new Ashéninka organisation and its allies at national level on the other, the process of legal demarcation was carried out. Between 1984 and 1988, 26 new Ashéninka communities were demarcated and titled in the zone, forming an almost continuous indigenous territory circumscribing the settler zone. These previously marginalised Indians had managed to organise and regain territorial control, thus curbing further colonist expansion[26]. The colonists were still in possession of vast areas of land for their cattle ventures, but their expansion and the influx of new settlers came to a halt, and the conflict was thus brought under control.

Colonist society was confused and unable to understand the success of the indigenous people at local and national level. The colonisation was now contained by a circle of bordering indigenous territorial properties, which could not be changed and which could be destroyed by neither intimidation nor violence. Their dream of expanding cattle farming to the ends of the earth had been destroyed and frustrations were great. Although that the economy continued to be based on a patron-peon relationship, it had narrow limits for its expansion and the Ashéninka were increasingly becoming an element of political force which nobody ever dreamed they could become. The symbolic highlight of the third defeat of "civilisation" came with the closure of the

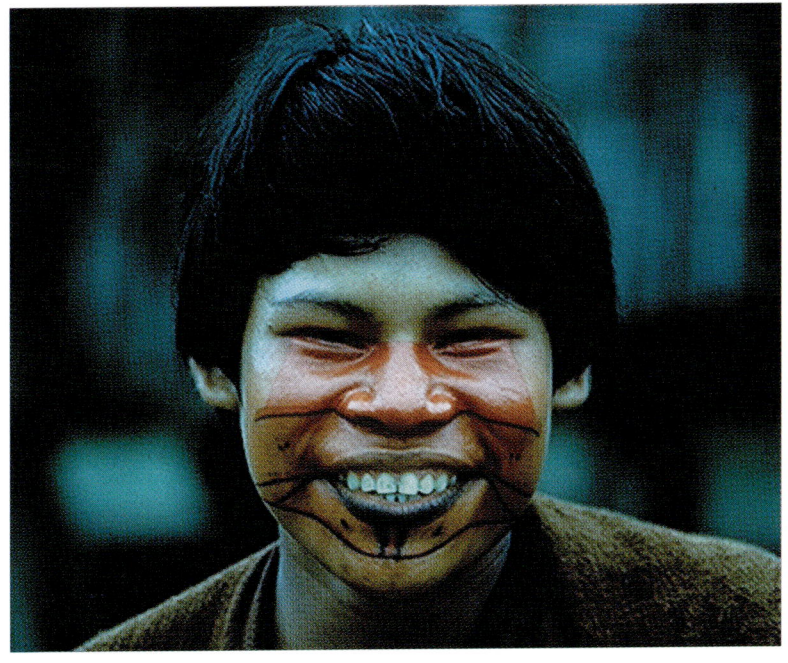

Catholic priesthood in Oventeni and the decay of the old church and mission.

III. The Second Phase - the Process in Atalaya

1. Notes and Questions from Atalaya

a. The Ucayali connection

During our work in Gran Pajonal, both the Ashéninka and the colonists constantly referred to the region of Atalaya. Many of the people of the Pajonal had worked for the Ucayali patrons for some time. Apparently these patrons had a greater selection of goods than the colonists in Oventeni and they were particularly well stocked with munitions and hunting weapons, which were much desired objects. There were three main trails used by the Indians which connected Gran Pajonal with the Upper Ucayali. One route went over the mountains from Oventeni and down to the mouth of the Unini river in the Ucayali. From there it was easy to obtain river transport upstream to Atalaya, but it was also possible to walk. The other trails went north of Gran Pajonal to the south of the Sira mountain and ended in Cocani and Chicosa (Catsingari) respectively, which are both minor secondary rivers flowing down into the Ucayali from the almost vertical mountainous wall which marks the border between Gran Pajonal and the Ucayali valley. These are old trading routes for the exchange of salt and metal tools between Ucayali and the Andes. To the extent that the slave trade partly emerged from these exchange systems, these routes were used in part by slave hunters on their correrías and in part for the transport of slaves on foot (see the next section on the history of Atalaya). Many of the largest farms were situated precisely at the mouths of the rivers where these trails finished, a conscious location which granted these patrons a certain control of the traffic and guaranteed them a stable supply of indigenous labour.

Stories were never lacking regarding the horrific working conditions which the indigenous lumberjacks suffered, but stories always become mixed with mythological tales of strange or spiritual events which had occurred to them during their stay inside the jungle. In this way, the Ashéninka constantly reproduced their own cosmology, rationality and universal order. Even the most primitive form of capitalist exploitation was integrated and destroyed in the logical universe of the Indians. Although the exploitation had always been understood as an expression of human perversion, in the narrative it was always placed within a parentheses of insignificance. The logic of capitalism had not penetrated. Thus it was difficult to collect truly informational material, although slowly a pattern was taking shape. The merchant's wife who took in boarders when we were in Oventeni was always telling stories about this and that, and added more pieces to this macabre puzzle. She remembered that her Spanish father had once been moved by an experience he had had when, after several days absence from his rubber processing camp, he returned and found all the indigenous labourers and other staff had been executed and their heads raised on posts. The crime had been committed by a rival patron. The story did not mention what reprisals were taken, but the woman knew that this sort of event was common in the province of Atalaya during the first decades of this century. She also remembered that as a young woman she had seen a river barge full of young indigenous women in Atalaya, which was preparing to leave. When she asked what was going on, she was told that they were being sent to Iquitos to be sold. This outraged her. There was confirmation from a number of sources that there had always been a constant traffic in young indigenous women for prostitution in Iquitos and, later, in Pucallpa. She also told that certain patrons had been involved in the traffic of women and children, also including colonists from Oventeni, but who had later moved on to the Ucayali. A number of current settlers in the Atalaya region were named.

My suspicions that the situation was not as historic as might at first be thought were reinforced one morning in July 1986. As part of our research plans, we had long ago decided to carry out a comparative survey in the Ucayali area to the south of Atalaya, in order record the frequency of contact, trading links, economic adaptations and the migratory routes between Gran Pajonal and Ucayali. Now we were going to make a short visit to Atalaya in order to establish the agreements and necessary contacts to take everything forward. A couple of days previously, a young Ashéninka woman had appeared at our house in Oventeni. She was one of those Indians who call themselves "civilised", that is, she wore the same clothes as settlers and spoke fluent Spanish. She was thirty four years old, and came with her son of 13 or 14. She asked us to help her obtain medicine for the child, who suffered from epilepsy. His medicine had run out and she could not get any more. Now his attacks had commenced once more and she was naturally very worried. She was also concerned as to whether the child would be able to continue his schooling because she wanted him to have all the opportunities that she never did. She knew that we were going to Atalaya, and believed that there was a place there where she could obtain the medicine. She actually came from Ucayali and had recently arrived in Gran Pajonal. She told us she had lived on a large farm for most of her life as a domestic servant and concubine of one of the well known patrons. She had originally been stolen from her parents during a correría in the Tambo River when she was scarcely four years old, and had been taken to Atalaya where she was sold. Later she went into the service of her boss, who was also the father of her son. Due to the boy's attacks, she and the child had been accused of witchcraft and everything bad that happened on the farm had become her fault[27]. Finally, the boss had threatened to kill her and her son and so she decided to flee to Gran Pajonal where she had some relations and where the boss feared to pursue her because of the fierce reputation of the Ashéninka. So she was now in Oventeni and glad that she had finally decided to escape. She found a solution to her problem of medicine and the story ended happily. The incident accentuated the actuality of the situation of slavery in Atalaya.

With respect to the image of the Ashéninka from Pajonal in national society as especially ferocious, their reactions in the face of unidentified "guests" must be seen in the light of the slave raids. The correrías did not belong to a distant past but were a cruel reality waiting at the next turn. I remember one occasion in the Tsiwanaski area of the Pajonal when we were living for a time with one of the local headmen. Suddenly a horn sounded and shortly afterwards the men began to shout out to the next hill. In a very short space of time a group of more than thirty men, armed with bows, arrows and shotguns, had been formed to link up with another similar group. The mobilisation was so rapid that the defence group almost seemed to rise up out of the earth. The reason was that the rumour had arrived that a group of unknown men had been seen at the headwaters of the Unini and it was expected that they were 'Ovayeris' who were hunting humans for the Atalaya patrons. They did not find the raiding party and the rumour was possibly a tall story. But awareness of the correrías is all too real.

b. Historic digression: The Adventist Mission
We arrived in Atalaya by boat, after an exploratory trip of one week from Puerto Ocopa downstream on the Tambo, and we stayed in the newest hotel in town. The small provincial town had grown substantially in the last ten years. There was quite a lot of river traffic and the medium sized container boats and floating sawmills were anchored near to the plaza. There were a lot more houses with zinc rooves, also more concrete buildings and it was clear that there was more money in circulation than ever. This economic boom was not the result of papaya production or cattle farming on the river banks. It was the result of the enormous growth in the illegal cultivation of coca and of the production of cocaine paste. In all the riverine zones of the Upper Ucayali, Urubamba and Tambo there were innumerable plantations, factories manufacturing cocaine paste and illegal landing strips. As Atalaya was

the junction of river traffic in these zones, it was also obvious that the town should come to operate as the service centre for this economy. The cocaine paste was produced through extraction with sulphuric acid, amongst other things, and the people involved in this production could always be identified because their nails were yellow and virtually eaten away by the acid. There were many men with short yellow nails in the bars of Atalaya. The motor launches, with newer and bigger outboard motors, dominated the riverine panorama and there were many light aircraft flying over the town. Economic growth had hit the small colonist town.

We had decided to stay for some months in the area downstream from Atalaya to carry out the comparative survey of the area around Unini, Chicosa and Cocani. I went to visit one of the more charismatic characters of the area, who lived in the Unini Mission, one of the small registered communities a little upstream in the Unini river. His name was Rufino Valles, he was an Ashéninka lay preacher and teacher at the Adventist Mission school which had founded the mission and community in 1937 as a mixed Piro-Asháninka settlement. Rufino had had a long and dramatic life. He had established the first Adventist Mission schools Tiaventeni and Pauti in Gran Pajonal in the 1960s. He had also been obliged to act as a guide for the anti-guerrilla corps "Los Rangers" when Lobatón's MIR front was defeated in Mapitzeviari. In gratitude, he was immediately arrested by the Republican Guard and accused of having been an accomplice of the guerrillas, since according to the intelligence services he knew too much about their activities. Nevertheless, he was freed shortly afterwards. Rufino's father had been one of the shamans of the area. He was originally from the Asháninka area which is upstream of the river Tambo, but he had converted to the Seventh Day Adventists during the time of the age old Asháninka movements which during the 1920s, 30s and 40s led to an indigenous exodus from the areas which had been invaded by the colonising front in Chanchamayo and Perené (cf. Barclay 1989, Bullon 1976, Elick 1968, Fernández 1986, Narby 1989, Stahl 1932, Veber 1991). Adventist millenarianism was a phenomenon which emerged with the arrival of the Peruvian Corporation in Perené. They had been allowed to missionise the Asháninka in exchange for pacifying and disciplining them as indentured labour for the Peruvian coffee plantations. They managed to concentrate the indigenous population in the concession area and provide the disciplined and cheap labour which the British company needed and which was difficult to obtain in the Andes. Stahl was a hardened opposer of the indigenous subsistence economy and the Ashéninka sustainable crop rotation system and promoted, in contrast, salaried work for the mission (that is, the Peruvian Corporation) or work for the local patrons (Veber 1991:74).

Slowly, contradictions between the mission's doctrine and the needs of the company owning the plantation emerged, which led to Stahl abandoning the concession area and moving firstly to Metraro where he continued his missionary work and later to Las Cascadas and Sutziki, in the Perené valley. These missions were battered by violent measles epidemics as was the camp of the Peruvian Corporation. The unhygienic conditions and dangers of contagion that the large concentrations of people brought about in the forest were also severely criticised by a Peruvian doctor who spent two years investigating the sanitary conditions in the company's colonies. He demonstrated that infant mortality was markedly higher in the missions than amongst the indigenous families who lived apart. He recommended that they returned to the traditional indigenous model of dispersed settlements and that a diverse subsistence production was reintroduced to counter the effects of the religious dietary taboos of the Adventist church. (Kuczynski-Godard 1939). A growing contradiction later emerged between the Asháninka who were members of the Adventist church and those who were not. Mutual accusations, threats and killing was becoming commonplace and there was a growing overall resistance to working for the plantation company and the patrons. In the end, there was no advantage of having them inside the Peruvian Corporation's colony and the mission was expelled in 1948 (Barclay 1989:128, Veber 1991:76). It was from this moment on that the great indigenous exodus towards Pichis, Tambo, Nevati, Ucayali and Urubamba began. It must be added that the great support which the Adventist Mission enjoyed amongst the Asháninka was based on the hope of a return of the Messiah and the restitution of the universal order for the Asháninka. Thus large groups of hopeful Asháninka had concentrated around Metraro and its surroundings, the area where Juan Santos Atahualpa had set up base with his movement less than 200 years earlier. They hoped that Stahl, in one way or another, would mediate the return. Several of the Asháninka who have taken on leadership positions within the indigenous movement over the last two decades grew up in and were educated by the Adventist mission. In spite of its economic and dogmatic strategy from a cultural point of view, the Adventist mission was for many years the only alternative if an indigenous person wished to obtain an education. Peruvian national society could only offer an education which was extremely authoritarian, hierarchical, racist and discriminatory, based solely on the premises of colonist society, in which an indigenous individual had not the slightest opportunity. Comparative studies and the school drop-out frequency confirm this situation (cf. Hanne Veber 1996). But the Messiah did not come and the Adventists lost their attraction. The role of offering an alternative education was then taken on by the evangelist Protestants of the USA and Europe. The most important of these missions was the Summer Institute of Linguistics which came down heavily on the side of a bilingual education and logistical support (cf. Hvalkof & Aaby 1981, Stoll 1985).

This Adventist indigenous movement led to the founding of several new indigenous communities, organised around Adventist worship. These new settlements were situated in Pichis, Nevati, Lower Tambo, Lower Urubamba and Upper Ucayali rivers, populated principally by Asháninka from Perené, but also by local Piro and Conibo. Unini was one of these Adventist indigenous communities close to one of the main trails between Gran Pajonal and Ucayali.

c. The frontier of civilisation: anecdotes of horror

In Unini I found Rufino Valles. He was very concerned about the developing situation, and told me that the situation and abuse in Ucayali against the indigenous population was possibly even worse than in Gran Pajonal. Later that day I returned to the banks of the Ucayali, where I was hoping to be able to stop a boat going upstream towards Atalaya, a journey of several hours. My timing was hopeless, there was no traffic on 29th of July on the Ucayali, the day after Peru's Day of Independence Today the whole province recovered from their hangovers of the previous day's festivities. Only one canoe with a slow 16 hp outboard motor puffed by, a so-called "peque". I signalled to them with my tee shirt, and although at first it seemed that they were going to pass by from afar, they suddenly turned and came in to the bank. In the canoe, an old dug-out, was a small group of people. Apart from the boat driver, there was a young Indian girl wearing a summer dress and a couple of young men, all Ashéninka. At the back end of the boat was a neat lady, clearly of European origin, dressed in clean jeans and a brightly flowered blouse. She was seated underneath an open black umbrella, to protect her from the burning sun. In the front of the canoe was seated a man of around 30 years of age, also with European features. He was wearing a pair of sun glasses with reflective lenses. Because of these, you could not see his eyes. He was not behaving in a particularly friendly way... After explaining where I had come from and where I was going, he invited me to go to with them to Atalaya in the canoe. When we got into the middle of the river, he began to question me on where I came from, what I was doing etc., etc. He also said that the only reason he had given me a lift was because he had never seen a "gringo" trying to stop a passing boat, and he wanted to find out what I was doing. I broadly explained what I was doing and that we had lived in Gran Pajonal for a long time, where we were still working. This made my host relax markedly. He introduced the lady as his aunt, Sra. E.S., and himself her nephew, Sr. C. D. patron and owner of an hacienda in Cocani. Both were relatives to one of the biggest and most notorious rubber barons of Ucayali and Urubamba, Sr. Carlos Scharff (see the historical summary which follows in the next chapter). It was obvious that I went up in his estimation when he heard that I lived amongst the "chunchos"[28] of Gran Pajonal. He told me that his father and grandfather had been the first colonists in Oventeni, before moving to Ucayali. It had been a golden age. His grandfather and father, together with the priest, had raped all of the young indigenous women in the area, he told me proudly - "hundreds of them, just like this one here" , he added pointing to the plump Asháninka girl sitting in the back end of the boat. She lowered her eyes shyly. None of the other indigenous people showed any sign of expression. The aunt smiled and murmured that certainly the grandfather and father had been very naughty. She commented that it was time to eat something and from a pot that was under a cloth in the bottom of the boat, she served roast chicken with cucumber salad and accompaniments. Very tasty. Tea was served from a thermos. Whilst we were eating and drinking, Don C.D. entertained me with more details about his grandfather's, father's and uncle's excesses, and of the trade in indigenous women and children. He had now arrived at the chapter concerning how many Campa men they had killed. For little reason, and often for no reason at all, he told me proudly. Loads of them. Why? Because that was how thing were in those days. But in the end it turned out badly, he added, because both his father and his uncle were finally murdered by the Indians. Both were killed in an ambush by the Amahuaca. Now he was continuing the proud tradition of his family, although he could not compete with all the exploits of his ancestors. He asked again exactly what I was doing when I carried out research of this kind, and I explained to him that, amongst other things, I was carrying out demographic surveys and that actually I was thinking of going to the Cocani area to visit the local Ashéninka. He looked at me pointedly and said that it could be dangerous and that I would have to take a lot of care there. Naively, I explained that in actual fact I knew the Ashéninka well, that I had contacts there and that, furthermore, I spoke enough Ashéninka to make myself understood, and thus I had absolutely no fear of any problems whilst visiting them in the Cocani area. This made him roar with laughter and exclaim that of course it was not the indigenous who were mortally dangerous. Cocani was a "zona roja"[29]. Coca crops and the production of paste, illegal pick-ups by small Colombian or Brazilian planes. They did not much like gringo visitors there. I emphasised that I was completely indifferent to the coca production, as long as I could carry out my survey. Difficult, he said, but perhaps possible. On arrival in Atalaya I received an invitation to visit him on his hacienda, if I wished. Unfortunately I never had the opportunity. But the words from the first time I arrived in this interesting colony in 1975 stood clear in my memory, "Welcome to the Republic of Atalaya".

We continued our exploratory trip, downstream of the Ucayali in a rusty version of Noah's Ark. An old iron river boat named "Pachacamilla", a typical construction on two levels which is very common in the waters of the Amazon, a flat bottom, a motor room at the back on the ground level, a large open storage area, a construction with six small cabins immediately behind the bridge and a large open room for passengers in the remainder of the upper floor with hooks where they could hang their hammocks. The boat was under the direction of one Captain Gómez, a large jovial river boatman with a cap, who I once promised to mention so that his name could appear in print in a book. So done. He was quite informative and I spent a lot of time on the bridge with him. The boat was full of all kinds of animals: pigs, cows, tortoises, turtles, iguanas, parakeets and parrots, monkeys large and small and aquarium fish in tanks. Apart from this there were all sorts of products from the forest: it was the season for tortoise eggs, a variety of dried vegetable products, tobacco, rice, beans and dried fish. Furthermore, a heavy cargo of bananas, water melons and other local products which the captain bought along the way from the local people who pile up their produce on the banks to be collected. Captain Gómez paid for the products in cash. This is a perfectly normal way of selling produce, although the price paid is very low, but payment is in cash and there are no economic problems of transport or an unresponsive market, nor the problems and expense of going to the large towns. Apart from this diverse cargo, noisy and smelly, there was an interesting mixture of passengers. Largely a mixture of local settlers and travelling salesmen of different ethnic origins, together with the usual school teachers going to Pucallpa to collect the wages which they had not received for more than three months because of "bureaucratic delays". There was the local artist, painter, poet and bard - a relative and nephew of aunt E.S. - who brought his guitar on the journey and every night he attracted the wrath of all the passengers by exercising his art in the company of a group of patrons with a passion for rum. There was one Asháninka boy of 12 or 13 years of age who was travelling as a stowaway. He had escaped from a Catholic mission on the river Tambo and was now paying for his voyage on the boat by working for the captain, who wanted to take him back to where he came from on the return voyage - perhaps. There was also an interesting group of young people who apparently shared a small cabin. We talked to them quite a lot. They were interested in what we were doing and we had long conversations with them regarding the possibilities for the Indians. In fact, they were so interested in the strategic scenarios we presented that they took notes in small books. Slowly we began to understand who they were. One of them one day explained to me that there was a determined group of school teachers from Ayacucho[30] who were also tired with the constant aggressions, abuses of power and misery and who had organised and taken things into their own hands. They mentioned no names. Yes, I had certainly heard talk of them. They later explained to me in detail what they had heard about their position. I explained that I was not really in agreement with the particular strategy and explained why, and particularly because cultural diversity did not allow for only a simplistic strategy. He proposed to hold a small meeting with a couple of his acquaintances on the boat, who should listen to my very interesting points of view. No sooner said than done. He then explained to me that the aforementioned group of Ayacucho school teachers had now become a movement and that they considered that the only thing they could do was to start everything from scratch. They wanted to put a brake on history and rewrite it from year zero. Everything prior to year zero would disappear and a new spirit and a new morale would be introduced. It seemed rather an ambitious project to me, which would demand fairly radical action. This was precisely what they had heard was being considered. They simply wanted to kill everyone bad and who thought wrongly. I asked them how they knew who was bad and who was good, but they demonstrated this through a complicated formula called the voice and opinion of the people, alias the Party. When I pointed out that this could well end up implicating more than half the Peruvian population, the reply was "yes". They were very happy that we had understood the message so quickly. And we had understood it.

At this time, Sendero Luminoso was becoming established along the Ucayali and the Urubamba and their tributaries. They were already well established in the zones of Tambo, Lower Perené and Ene-Apurimac where they controlled the river traffic, attracted by the enormous economic potential which the cocaine economy offered. The MRTA[31] was at the same time trying to establish itself in the larger cities but also had ambitions in the rural areas. As is known, there was a war between the two subversive organisations and the first territorial conflicts were appearing. Nevertheless, there was no apparent State intervention and the army was absent, in general terms. But as we shall see, this was only the calm before the storm.

d. The end of the beginning and vice versa

After this eventful exploratory trip in the Republic of Atalaya we returned to Gran Pajonal to finalise our work there. But it was a long and hard fight to carry forward the demarcation of the first 24 communities there and there was a latent tension whilst this was going on. The

Oventeni cattle farmers were using all kinds of tricks to try to stop the work and at one point, in November 1986, the two groups were on the point of entering into an armed conflict. The director of the Ministry of Agriculture's office in Satipo, who was of the opinion that the indigenous population was a threat to progress, was a faithful ally of the Oventeni colonists and did all he could to put a stop to the demarcation process. At the same time he was furious at having been sidelined by the Special Project - PEPP. Firstly, he tried to get in ahead of the demarcation process by coming to an agreement with the settlers which consisted of his office demarcating the settlers' property in exchange for a per metre payment. The work began, paid by the settlers themselves, but it did not get very far because of a lack of labour. Then he tried to convince the Ashéninka to provide the labour (sic!) and when their leader, Miguel Camaiteri, refused he tried to bring him down through a manipulation of the "divide and rule" type. Firstly he got an indigenous leader from the neighbouring organisation CART[32] to try to get the OAGP to withdraw from AIDESEP and join a rival national organisation, which apparently they could manipulate better. When this did not work, the same director came to Gran Pajonal from Satipo with a letter from the same CART dirigente, H.P., who was presented as the "top Asháninka dirigente" and which overruled and took away all authority from the OAGP dirigente, Miguel Camaiteri, and told the Ashéninka to help the colonists in their counter-demarcation. They were also informed that there had been an agreement with the PEPP to do things in this way and that the indigenous demarcation would be suspended. Although the colonists applauded this energetically, but naturally no Ashéninka believed it and Miguel Camaiteri consequently repelled the coup attempt and the lies. Tension grew whilst the arrival of the PEPP surveyors was awaited.

Nevertheless, nobody could understand what made a CART Asháninka act in this way. But there was an invisible wild card in the game which became apparent later on. Sendero Luminoso had drawn up a secret plan to convert Gran Pajonal into the centre for food supplies for its operations in Ucayali, Tambo and Pichis. So they were in no way interested in the idea of the Asháninka, who were neither cattle farmers nor peasants, taking control of the territory and they were fully aware that OAGP was not a potential ally. It must be remembered that Sendero Luminoso fully identified with the colonist culture, from which at this time it recruited most of its converts. Furthermore, there would be no need for private property, not even in the form of private collective property, when the new State appropriated all the means of production and the land. Thus in the eyes of Sendero Luminoso, indigenous land titling was a waste of time and effort. And there was general consensus on this in colonist Satipo. Sendero Luminoso had already established itself in the zone of Tambo and was exercising violent pressure over the CART dirigentes. H.P. had thus been recruited to the force as a liaison and supplies agent and he had been allocated the task of preventing the advance of OAGP in Gran Pajonal. Many of the CART dirigentes were assassinated by the subversive organisation in the following years, including H.P.[33] But the determination of the people of Gran Pajonal and their leaders bore fruit. The surveyors arrived and revealed the fraud. The trained officials of the PEPP who carried out the work and the Ministry of Agriculture official of the office of Native Communities in Lima intervened at the last moment and explained to the Oventeni colonists that the Ashéninka in actual fact had right on their side. Their new organisation, OAGP, was greatly strengthened through this process and the person responsible for the community demarcation in the organisation, Miguel Camaiteri, carried out exceptional work in spite of the massive opposition and threats with which he was constantly faced. The surveyors began their work of demarcation and we provided, at the written request of the PEPP, aerial photographs, detailed maps and technical information which was not preciously available. The demarcation now continued normally and the first phase was carried out during the course of 1987.

But what would happen after the demarcation and titling? How would the indigenous territory be consolidated and how would the process towards development, self-management and a sustainable Ashéninka economy be continued? It was clear that on the one hand there was no guarantee unless the neighbouring areas, in particular Atalaya and Ucayali, were also pacified through a reorganisation of land ownership, and that on the other hand it was completely impossible if the indigenous organisations were not significantly strengthened as autonomous political players at all levels. We began Slowly to elaborate the idea of a general coordination of work and a widening of the process of land titling including the area of Atalaya.

After concluding our work in Gran Pajonal in the spring of 1987, we moved on to the native community of Unini and the native community of Chicosa respectively, to continue the work in Ucayali. During this work we became well and truly aware of how dreadful the situation was. In the area of Unini, practically all the families had experienced abuse at the hands of the patrons. On the one hand the Unini area, as already mentioned, had been one of the preferred zones for correrías by the patrons and recruitment of cheap labour through debt bondage, and on the other hand there were still valuable lumber resources in the area which the patrons were illegally extracting. Naturally, this was also being done with indigenous labour gained through confidence tricks and debts.

What people told us during our survey was not inconsequential. The very same Rufino Valles had lost a son the previous year. He had disappeared during work in the forest for one of the patrons, who could not explain how he had disappeared and denied all responsibility. Don Rufino had notified the authorities of the situation but all he got was a shrug of the shoulders. Disappearances were the normal order of things. So were crude violence and sexual abuse. As the local Ashéninka from around Unini found out that we were carrying out a census and interviewing people about the work situation, many people came forward wanting to tell about the abuses to which they had been subjected. A neighbour from the other side of the river told how, under threat of death, he had been forced to witness the patron rape his wife. Others told how they had seen sick and exhausted people brutally assassinated by the patrons whilst working in lumber extraction because they could not keep up the rhythm of work. How they had to live on a bag of manioc flour a day when they were working in the forest, how their lands were invaded and their crops stolen, how they were permanently enslaved because of debts, how their children were taken away from them and sent as child labour for the patrons, how the colonist authorities refused to register them as Peruvian citizens and refused to give them any personal identification documents. It is impossible to travel anywhere in Peru without your identity document. It is illegal and dangerous. Apart from the fact that people without personal documents obviously do not exist also have no rights.

They told about the extensive trade in children, women and entire families. One name which was mentioned several times as one of the fat cats of this trade, and in Gran Pajonal too, was "Manquishu", the one armed. He was one of the first settlers in the area and began his career in Oventeni. It seemed that correrías and the human Slave trade had been one of his specialities. Now he was Lieutenant Governor in the neighbouring village of Diamante Azul[34]. Appointed as representative of the President of the Republic and guarantor of the fulfilment of the Peruvian constitution. An honourable man. There were many such honourable men amongst the patrons of the area. During a survey trip along the river Unini it was confirmed that the correrías and forced recruitment of workers were not things of the past. We made several of these survey trips together with Don Rufino and a neighbour. At one point we arrived at a settlement, not far from Unini, but when we got out of the boat and climbed up the river bank towards the houses, not a soul was to be seen. You could see that people had been there recently, fires were smoking, there were a number of tools and there was a spinning wheel with cotton thread which had recently been used. But not a soul. Our accompaniers said they had obviously fled, but that all we had to do was wait and they would return. And so we began to shout explaining why we had come. And one by one they appeared from the nearby forest and fields. Firstly the older children, then the women and little ones. There were no adult men. When we explained who we were and what we were going to do, we were invited in and offered a little maniok and roast gourds. They told us that they had thought it was a correría when they heard the sound of the motor and the children had seen that we were gringos. When we returned to Unini we found out that "Manquishu" had been to visit with a group of settlers with clubs to beat me up, to make me leave the area. But when they heard that we had travelled upstream towards Gran Pajonal, they had given up waiting for me. The patrons then tried to spread the rumour that I was "pishtaco", a white devil who kills indigenous women by cutting their throats and then taking out their fat. The fat is later sold to make the gringos' machines work. This is an old Andean legend about colonialism and exploitation which is widespread in Peru. In a version I heard, it were satellites which were powered by human fat. Others, with more secular interpretations, said that it was for the perfume industry[35]. But the patrons did not manage to put a stop to the process.

In the weeks that followed, Ashéninkas wanting to contribute to the census and to set up their own communities study flocked to the Unini community. Don Rufino was delighted because finally he could see that something was happening, which he interpreted as divine intervention, something which no-one will ever know. We helped to complete a series of requests for the registration and demarcation of new communities and went to Lima with a stack of applications and accompanying documentation under the arm.

e. The initial intervention

In Lima I got in touch with the office for Native Communities of the Ministry of Agriculture. Whilst I was sitting in the waiting room, someone else appeared, who I did not know but who had the features of an Asháninka. He sat down on another chair and, like me, had a pile of official letters under his arm. When the head of the office, Sra. Camargo came out to greet us, she smiled and introduced us. The other person was Sr. Miqueas Mishari, one of the dirigentes of AIDESEP and later to be that organisation's president. He had come for exactly the same reason as I, that is, to exert pressure with the aim of obtaining the demarcation and titling of the area around Atalaya. In particular the two communities of Tahuanti and Sabaluyo were having enormous problems which had now escalated into violent clashes and attacks on heads of communities. Sr. Mishari and I had a long conversation about the overall situation in Atalaya and Ucayali and he was very interested in beginning a process of demarcation in the area of Unini. He was an Adventist, he knew the Unini Mission and had been there recently. The inhabitants of Unini had also mentioned his name on a number of occasions as someone to be trusted and who they hoped would help them. He was extremely well respected in the communities. The Ministry of Agriculture also wanted to help, but they had only limited resources for a demarcation project such as this. "Limited resources" normally meant that it could not be carried out and would get lost in the labyrinths of bureaucracy. But they were obliged to deal with the concrete conflict in Tahuanti and Sabaluyo, and our joint complaints regarding the innumerable abuses being committed in the area also made the head of the office react. AIDESEP had also become increasingly committed to the situation in Atalaya throughout 1987. After a number of visits to Atalaya, where the horrifying information continued to increase, the first step towards official intervention was taken. At the end of the year, a multisectoral commission reporting to the Ministry of Justice was set up to investigate the assertions regarding the terrible abuses (see the article of the then legal advisor to AIDESEP, Sr. Pedro García, in this publication pages 15-80 on the work of the commission and its report). During the development of this process in 1987, a new indigenous organisation emerged in the province of Atalaya, OIRA, which came to play a determining role in indigenous organisation in the Upper Ucayali and in the subsequent land titling project.

Whilst all this was going on, we continued our work in Ucayali. Now we had moved to the native community of Chicosa which was situated some hours by "peque" down river from Unini. Chicosa was a former missionary station of the North American evangelists of the South American Mission (SAM), a conservative and fundamentalist organisation.One morning towards the end of September (1987) a couple of agitated Ashéninkas came looking for me. I had to go down to the river immediately because something had happened. It was important. Down by the river there was a small crowd. There were a number of inhabitants from the community, including the indigenous authorities of Chicosa, who were gesticulating. In the river there were a couple of wooden boats with powerful Johnson motors and next to them, on the bank, two policemen armed with powerful military carbines. In front of them was standing an old acquaintance, Sra. E.S. She shook my hand, smiling. Between the two groups an extremely thin Ashéninka man was standing, with a handkerchief on his head. According to her, he had escaped from her hacienda and had sought refuge in Chicosa. He owed her a lot of work for some goods that she had already given him, pots and other cooking utensils, a number of metres of cotton material, salt and shotgun shells. His verbal contract established that he should work until they had been paid for, but now he had fled. And it was the second time he had tried to get out of his debt. The Chicosa authorities were clearly nervous at the presence of the Guards and said nothing but stared fixedly at me. The thin man said nothing either, but kept his gaze on the ground. I gave a long speech on the fact that nobody could stop anyone from abandoning their work if they wanted to. That according to the constitution all citizens were free and could move freely wherever they wanted. That nobody could be detained because of debts. That Slavery, including debt Slavery, had been abolished last century and that, furthermore, according to Peruvian labour law it was totally prohibited to use "debt bondage" and pay in advance for labour services, that they had no right to detain him since he had committed no criminal act and that, apart from all this, we lived in a civilised world in 1987 (a rather absurd argument, given the situation!) and that Peru had signed various agreements and international declarations prohibiting this sort of thing. "But Sr. Gringo, he is an Indian and in debt to me! He will not be detained, I merely want to take him back to my farm so that he works for what he owes me." I obviously could well see that it was reasonable. We were civilised. It was clear that my moralising speech had not impressed her. I said that if she had a complaint, she should go to the police or the judge in Atalaya and she could thus place a civil request. Sra. E.S. shook her head. Now she brought forward a Guard and politely noted that in actual fact they had a summons from the judge. I asked to see it and they handed me a folded piece of paper on which was typed that an order for the arrest of a native by the name of Sargento had been issued because he owed work to the estate of Sra. Scharff. Signed by the Atalaya judge and stamped accordingly. I could not believe my own eyes, but the document was apparently genuine. The thin man tried to say that this was not his name, but nobody was listening. In view of the legal writ and the armed guards it seemed impossible to prevent the arrest. But at least we could prevent him from being taken back to the woman's estate, where the treatment he would be given was foreseeable. Thus, I insisted that he should be brought before a judge in Atalaya. After some discussion, the guards accepted this. At that time we knew that the commission and the AIDESEP lawyer would be in Atalaya precisely on that day to receive denunciations regarding different abuses. It was important that the case should be presented to the commission and the lawyer so that they could intervene with the Atalaya authorities.

In order to make sure that, in any case, he was not taken back to the estate, the guards agreed that the Chicosa indigenous authorities should accompany them to Atalaya, since it was in Chicosa that he had sought refuge. The problem was that there was no space in their boat. Another boat was found and some fuel bought so that they could accompany the prisoner. The small convoy then set off upstream of the Ucayali headed for Atalaya. I was later told that the case was indeed presented to the AIDESEP commissions lawyer, and that after long discussions with the judge, they managed to free Sargento. (Cf., García p. in this volume) In spite of all the precautions, he had been burnt on the face with cigarettes on the way to Atalaya. We were glad that he was not sent back to the hacienda.

We were naturally enthusiastic about the fact that AIDESEP now actively intervened in the case and it seemed that at last the situation had become known outside of a closed circle. Perhaps it would be possible to get higher authorities involved in some way. Public attention regarding the problems, could, at least, tone down the patrons actions. But we were fully convinced that it was absolutely necessary to carry out an immediate demarcation and titling of the indigenous territories so that the indigenous population could have a real opportunity of changing their situation. It also seemed important that there should be a certain consensus or at least mutual comprehension and communication amongst the different players, both indigenous and non-indigenous, who were working in the area, be they missionary organisations, development NGOs, researchers or other individuals, the Ministry of Agriculture and the authorities of the education and health sectors etc., as well as the most important of all, the indigenous organisations.

To begin this process, we organised two meetings in Lima on the experience of Gran Pajonal. The meetings were on purpose held on "neutral political ground" so that everyone could participate without "ideological" problems[36]. The aim of the meetings was to act as the starting point of a coordinating initiative and a debriefing on our research project. Nearly all the organisations and institutions working in the native communities of the area participated in the meetings and the idea was initially merely to coordinate activities to avoid double or parallel work and, furthermore, to give the indigenous organisations an opportunity to gain information on the confusing maze of interested organisations. The participation of AIDESEP was crucial for the future consolidation of the process. The meetings were held in August and October of 1987. The first meeting was held before the commission had begun its work in Atalaya and the second immediately after it had begun the documentation work. The outline of a proposal for a programme of ethno-development had been drawn up for the last meeting as an introduction to a plan of action (Hvalkof 1987b), and other participants presented short written proposals for future activities[37]. It was during these meetings that it was proposed that the positive results of the land titling process in Gran Pajonal should be replicated in Ucayali through a similar, but wider, project. This was emphasised even more by the growing conflict between colonists and natives which was developing in two communities close to Atalaya, Tahuanti and Sabaluyo, in which AIDESEP had become involved. It was also during these meetings that an outline proposal for the establishment of a large protected area in the Sira mountains, to the north of Gran Pajonal, in the form of a Reserva Comunal[38] was presented. Nevertheless, there was still no concrete proposal as to how a project of this kind could be financed and implemented. But the proposal was still very much in the air.

In 1988, the multisectoral commission published its initial report (AIDESEP 1988a, 1988b, 1991a, 1991c; Gray and Hvalkof 1990a, 1990b) and in 1989 the Instituto Indigenista Peruano (IIP) published the commission's final report and recommendations (IIP 1989). It was a terrifying testimony to the serious crimes which were occurring, ranging from multiple murder, disappearances, torture, assault and battery, Slavery, abduction of children, rape and other sexual abuses, to a series of infringements of labour laws and agrarian and forestry legislation (García p. 55-74 in this volume). With few exceptions, all of the accused were local patrons and allied authorities ranging from the forestry service to the police and even the justice of the peace. In all, 17 of the local patrons, and 3 major regional lumber patrons were accused of more than 60 criminal counts. (None of the accused were ever trialed.) Nevertheless, the commission's investigation only revealed the tip of the iceberg.

2. Looking Back over History

a. The idiosyncratic foundation of Atalaya

When one looks back on the events and the alarming information which exists, one can but wonder how the slave trade, chattle slavery, debt bondage and the innumerable abuses could develop and continue until only a few years ago without anyone doing anything about it. It is particularly striking since many well known reports existed, travel accounts and research work in Ucayali, Urubamba and Gran Pajonal which documented these outrages from before the rubber boom and practically up until today[39]. It is even more striking when one considers that during the last 50 years many foreign and Peruvian researchers have visited the area and that missionaries from different churches, beliefs and missionary organisations (e.g. Evangelists, Protestants, Seventh Day Adventists, Mennonites) lived for a long time in the area, and that they were in the front line observing these outrages and they had direct knowledge of them. One can add to this various Peruvian NGOs and of course the civil authorities, health and education ministries and departments. There also exists newer information relating to the same.

Miguel Camaiteri with rescued orphans

Some anthropologists in particular have described the conditions. One of the first to publish information in this respect was John Bodley (1970, 1972) and various others followed him more recently (eg d'Ans 1981, Schäfer 1988, Gow 1991). But one swallow does not make a summer. This was information contained within anthropological studies and ethnographic descriptions aimed basically at an intellectual audience abroad and, as such, formed part of academic discourse. It was very far from the political processes which could resolve the situation. This is not meant as a criticism of these researchers. On the contrary, they have made a significant and well documented contribution to bringing to light and doing away with these conditions through their excellent work. But it brought about no action or reaction per se. Although the information existed, until the publication of the commission's report, no complete and focalised documentation had been presented within the Peruvian public sphere.

We have often raised questions about the lack of intervention on the part of the non-Catholic missionaries who lived there[40]. Amongst others, we put the problem to a sympathetic and elderly couple of Mennonites who had worked for a generation in the Atalaya area. They confirmed that our experiences in Unini and Chicosa were not exceptional but rather typical of the relationships between patrons and indigenous labourers. They added innumerable stories and anecdotes of the same kind. Their spontaneous explanation as to why they themselves, for example, had not radically intervened can be summed up as a) that they had instead tried to intervene and mediate on a personal level, talking to the patrons when there were conflicts, and thus softening the effects, b) that there was no public structure in Atalaya, or in Peru as a whole, which dealt with this sort of thing, c) that their mission was work of spiritual Christian motivation and that they were not in a position which would permit them to judge the others' actions (although of course they had many moral criteria regarding what was right and wrong), d) that in local Latin American Catholic society there was much scepticism regarding evangelist gringos, which would probably result in their expulsion from the area if they intervened directly and complained and that this would be to betray their Christian mandate. However, they added that in reality they wished that an end could be put to the outrages and that more tolerable conditions were developed. I received similar arguments from other missionaries, in which one missionary added that her organisation was not prepared to take on responsibility for this type of politicised issue and that she simply lacked the contacts which we had with respect to the rights of indigenous peoples and the possibilities of intervening. She added that she wished she had them. It is clear that no immediately accessible forum or network existed amongst the different people and institutions which could have facilitated common action. The different policies and ideologies prevented this. But it still does not explain why many Peruvian institutions, organisations and individuals which have worked and lived in the area, did nothing. There are a number of possible reasons: a) that they simply did not realise how serious the situation was or the magnitude of the exploitation and abuses, b) that nobody wanted to risk a conflict with the settlers and local patrons on whom they depended socially and organisationally, c) that they did not want to recognise the magnitude of the problem because personally they could not bear the consequences of a clash with friends and acquaintances in Atalaya society, d) that even if they intervened, they would have no means of breaking the power relations and hierarchy, and so intervention would probably only have led to the downfall of the person himself or his/hers organisation. Thus the status quo of power relations was only confirmed.

But the Indians themselves, the victims, where were they in this process? Given the state of affairs, it is clear that they had absolutely no-one to turn to and nowhere to denounce their suffering until an indigenous organisation was established and until they became aware of the importance of this and that they had civil rights and the right to protest. Here we come to the crux of the matter: the conditions in Ucayali had existed for so long - for several generations - that the situation was normal. This was the way things had always been. "It just was like this" as the patron had expressed it - the idiosyncrasy of Atalaya. Atrocities and exploitation were so engrained both in indigenous and non-indigenous society and in the collective "memory", that nothing fundamentally bad could be seen in it. Until it was suddenly unveiled with the publication of the commission's report and its political follow up on the part of the indigenous organisations. A sort of "emperor's new clothes" syndrome. But to understand how it got to this point, it is necessary to outline the economic and geographical history of the Upper Ucayali.

b. The social structures of extraction

Since the navigation of the river by the first Europeans, the driving force behind the colonisation of Ucayali was the extraction of a number of different natural products with the aim of marketing them, both on the national market and for export. In the lowest areas of the Ucayali River basin, the extractivist economy was Slowly being formed throughout the 18th century. Extraction of the Zarzaparilla root (Smilax sp.) and bark from the Cinchona tree (Cinchona officinalis), also known as Quina or Cascarilla, both for medicinal purposes (anti-syphilitics and quinine) was beginning. Other products of early interest were dried and salted fish, palm fibres and hats made of the same, exotic animals, skins and feathers. Logistic limitations still made the Indians, with their canoes, the masters of this area. Nevertheless, it also made them obvious targets as indentured labour in the emerging extractivist economy. The idiosyncratic foundation of the dominant society's rapport with the indigenous population for the next centuries was created during this period.

Historically, the extractivist economy of the Amazon has been characterised by recurrent cycles of boom and bust, related to specific products. It reached its climax with the rubber boom of the first decades of this century, opening the way for permanent settlements around trading posts. The social relations of the extractivist production in Peru have from the beginning been characterised by exploitation of the knowledge and labour of the Indians, procured by local patrons through debt bondage and indentured labour. Debts were, and still are, established through advance payment in kind to the indigenous worker. This method is known in Spanish as "enganche", meaning to "hook up" or "hitch a horse to a carriage". The system is well known from the haciendas in the Andean highland and from the agricultural corporations in the montaña. In the Upper Amazon, this developed into a particular system of accumulation known as the system of "habilitacion", which has been the motor of the extractivist economy. The 'habilitation' system functions as a hierarchy of interconnected debt relations in a chain of exploitation. At the top of the system, the exporter or commercial house prepays a contractor to deliver the product by a specified time. He in turn prepays or 'habilitates' several subcontractors, who 'habilitate' local patrons, etc. At the bottom of the chain we reach the ultimate producer, generally an Indian and his family. The related system of slavery developed, overlapping the debt bondage system. Since debts were passed on from father to son, debts were accumulated through generations. Indebted indigenous families became real capital or property owned by the patrons, a commodity that could be traded on the market.

This commodification of the indigenous population rapidly evolved into a real slave trade run by the contractors involved in extractive enterprises. With further colonisation and with changes in production and labour requirements, the traffic in slaves became rampant in the Upper Amazon and developed into an independent economic activity, an 'extractive' industry in its own right. Armed slave raiding, so called 'correrías', became widespread and markets for Indian Slaves developed in the few commercial centres of the Upper Amazon. During the short peak period of the rubber bonanza, 1890-1915, hundreds of thousands of Indians were enslaved as rubber tappers in rubber extraction. The atrocities committed by the rubber barons were numerous. Some cases are well documented, such as the notorious Putumayo scandal, where the London-based Peruvian Amazon Company Inc. was responsible for the cruel deaths of some 30,000 Indians in the extraction of 4,000 tonnes of raw rubber. And the Putumayo was just one rubber concession in one river area (Hardenburg 1913, State Department of the USA 1913, Valcárcel 1915, Taussig 1984, 1985; Gray 1990, Hvalkof 1998a). In the Ucayali basin, the notorious rubber baron, Carlos Fermín Fitzcarraldo, maintained a similar regime of horror although the atrocities committed here were never exposed through a systematic inquiry like the Putumayo scandal. As we shall see, slavery and the trade in Indian individuals as well as entire families, persisted in the Atalaya province of the Upper Ucayali until as recently as 1988 (Hvalkof 1994b, Gray 1997, Renard-Casevitz 1980).

The sudden collapse of the rubber economy after 1914 paralysed the commercial and economic system of the Peruvian Amazon. The rubber firms went bankrupt over night and many individual patrons fled the region to escape their debts. Large numbers of indigenous peons suddenly found themselves free, left on their own in foreign areas where their patrons had brought them to collect rubber. Some of the more industrious and optimistic patrons and colonists stayed and began to look for new economic opportunities and alternative products to extract. Lumber became the next major target[41]. During the rubber boom's hunt for growth to tap, the rubber gatherers had been driven into the most inaccessible corners of the Amazon forest. This accumulated knowledge of the area's geography and forest composition gave the patrons an enormous advantage in lumber extraction[42]. The expanding agricultural frontier in the montaña had created a growing market for boards and building materials and the export market for tropical hard woods was beginning to develop in the lower regions. The first export company for tropical hard woods was established in Iquitos in 1918, exporting whole trunks to the USA (San Ramón 1975:171) and the first sawmill started operating in 1920 (ibid: 171, Santos & Barcley 1995, Malleux 1986). Spurred on by a Peruvian law of 1930 which prohibited the export of gross and undressed hard woods (San Ramón 1975: 171), the new industry grew rapidly. The number of saw mills in 1981 totalled some 400[43] (Malleux 1986:275)

Lumber extraction is as dependent on indigenous knowledge and labour as rubber gathering was and the social relations of production established during the previous extractivist periods, that is, the system of debt bondage through "habilitación" have been maintained by the patrons. Lumber extraction is still the most (and perhaps the only) lucrative business in the Atalaya province apart from crude oil which is the most recent extractivist boom, but which is not labour intensive and, furthermore, is in the hands of multinational and foreign based oil companies. Thus the lumber industry is highly dependent on indigenous labour and access to the indigenous territories, creating an obvious motivation for lumber patrons to invest in counteracting indigenous organisation, land titling and democratisation.

c. The historic construction of Slavery

The first attempt to colonise Ucayali was in 1641, when three Franciscans navigated the Perené-Tambo until they reached Ucayali, where according to missionary sources they were martyred by the Conibo close to the mouth of the Aguaytia river. The precise place of this first clash, and the reason for it, is not known.

The next attempt was in 1685-86, when German Jesuits from Mainas (the area in which the current Iquitos is situated) navigated up river by the Ucayali to set up in a fair sized Conibo village and the middle Ucayali. The place was called San Miguel. A couple of months later, Spanish Franciscans sailed down river by the Perené and by chance also stopped in San Miguel (thus baptised on this occasion). The enterprising Conibo then examined which of the two orders could offer better metal tools and merchandise in general and as the Franciscans were in a position to offer more than the Jesuits (who had temporarily journeyed back to get more merchandise) the Conibo granted them the "mission concession". (Ortiz 1974:74-76). It emerges from sources that at this time there already existed quite a trade in metal tools and salt in Ucayali. In the descriptions it also emerges that the Asháninka with roots in the culture of Gran Pajonal were at that time living in the area down river of Atalaya, but in general there was a lot of movement and trade in both directions on the river. We are also informed that there was quite a lot of piracy and conflict between the different local indigenous groups, as a consequence of the introduction of European merchandise and in particular metal tools and arms, which were much in demand, and this apparently dislocated the existing balance of power. The simultaneous offer made by the Jesuits and the Franciscans to the Conibo of San Miguel also caused a conflict between the two orders regarding which had the greater right to proselytise and settle in Ucayali. Thus the European colonisation of the Upper Ucayali began with power struggles and a policy of "divide and rule", each religious order with its military garrison of Spanish soldiers and each with its indigenous sympathisers (Ibid 77-79). It should also be mentioned that the same year a young Jesuit who went up river to preach was killed by Piro in the Tambo river. This led both missions to plot a punitive military expedition in the zone of Atalaya against the Piro, who they wanted to destroy (Ibid. 79). In the plan it was also included that the Conibo, who already had trading controversies with the Piro and the Ashéninka, would help them teach the Piro a "lesson" (ibid). Thus power relations, violence and interethnic conflict were established from the very start in the Upper Ucayali.

The conflicts, repression and epidemics which followed the Europeans caused the first indigenous uprising of importance in Upper Ucayali in 1695 which, with the death of the driving force of the Jesuit Mission, Father Richter, momentarily halted the colonisation and put a permanent halt to the Jesuit dream of gaining control in the Upper Ucayali, Urubamba and Tambo. The Franciscans established themselves 50 years later further down the Ucayali but the rebellion of Juan Santos Atahualpa in the central jungle in 1742 stopped the expansion, and later the Setebo, under the command of the "cacique" (headman) Runcato, rose up in Lower Ucayali in 1766 where they destroyed all the Franciscan missions. Upper Ucayali had been a zone closed to Europeans for many years. The Selva Central and Gran Pajonal were equally inaccessible, but in 1791 the Franciscans managed to establish a mission once again in Sarayacu, close to Contamana and in the years up to 1817, the Franciscans managed to found 9 new missions in Upper Ucayali of which one, of the name Lima-Rosa de los Piros (also: Santa Rose de los Piros), is located close to the actual location of Atalaya. The secular motivation was to establish a logistical link between the coast and the mountain and down to the navigable part of the Amazon in order to be able to realise the old dream of great colonisation, development and trade. Between 1816 and 1820, the route Andamarca-Pangoa-Tambo-Ucayali was travelled along there and back seven times with no problems, which at the time was a great event. In the mission hopes for the future were enormous.

But then the Peruvian war of independence and the establishment of the new Peruvian State got in the way. The Franciscans were forced to abandon the country for a while and give up their civilising venture. A curious anecdote illustrates how great the communications problems between Lima and the Andes/Amazon were at this time: Father Plaza, who was the energetic leader of the Saracayu mission, to the northeast of Gran Pajonal, amongst the Pano speakers, remained completely isolated during the war of independence. Father Plaza continued alone, with no contact to the Franciscans, for the next 30 years in Saracayu. The economy of the mission was based on sugar and zarzaparilla production which was bartered in Brazil in exchange for tools and other necessities, completely isolated from the new Peruvian State and the national economy. However, he was "rediscovered" when the return of the Franciscans was permitted.

But meanwhile other initiatives were underway. The foreign markets of North America and Europe had begun to look longingly at South American products, particularly medicinal plants and exotic goods. The great boost for the extractivist economy came with the logistics revolution which the introduction of steam ships caused in the middle of the 1850s. The first extractivist boom in Ucayali was the zarzaparilla root (Simlax sp.) firstly for medicinal purposes and then for making drinks. Zarzaparilla is having another revival and can now be bought in capsule form in health shops throughout America and Europe. Another extremely profitable export good was the "Panama hats" which are not from Panama but Peru and Ecuador, plaited with fibres from the bombonaje palm. The method of gaining these products was through "habilitation", as previously explained, and other forms of Slavery, and the Slaves became another extractive product in this new economy. During the same period the Franciscans also returned to establish the Santa-Rosa mission in Atalaya in 1879. They managed to bring together a large group of Piro and Ashéninka but the head of the mission came into conflict with the traders and patrons, who threatened to kill him, and the mission was again abandoned in 1881. From this time on, the patrons had a free rein and they established the order of the day without restrictions up until the present day.

With the best logistical and economic possibilities, the Amazon became an interesting area for the new Peruvian State, and geopolitical interests, tributes and control led to the establishment of the navy, with two gunboats on the Amazon and the Ucayali. Peru thus expressed its new national presence through the first State massacre on Indians in Ucayali. On 10th December 1866, the Peruvian navy, with gunboats El Morona, El Napo and El Putumayo, carried out a decisive punitive expedition against the Cashibo indigenous at Chonta Isla, at the mouth of the river Pachitea, in the Ucayali. The cause was an armed clash at the beginning of the year when El Putumayo had to seek refuge in the place due to running aground. According to historical sources, the officers Sr. Tavara and Sr. West disembarked and took a few bananas from an Indian field without asking. They were attacked on the return and killed by the owners of the field, local Cashibo (Uni).

During the punitive expedition, the navy attacked the Cashibo hamlet and took the women and children prisoner, to later be sold as slaves in Iquitos. This was a consciously chosen form of revenge. In a desperate attempt to free the women and children, some 500 Cashibo men attacked the commando group on its return to the gunboats from the beach, where hundreds of Cashibo men were mercilessly massacred by the artillery of the war ships (for a detailed description see d'Ans 1982:161-162).

The work force in the form of slaves had at this time been converted into a commodity as part of the economy of the region. The correrías after indigenous slaves were common in all parts and involved all of the indigenous groups of the Ucayali. With the booming economy of rubber extraction, in 1880 human exploitation and perversion reached new heights. The Franciscan father, Luis Sabaté, carried out an expedition in Urubamba and Ucayali in 1874 and described the situation in Upper Urubamba as follows:

> That day the Piro went on a correría against the Campa and took many things. It was one of those surprise attacks which the savage tribes make against each other, when they are at war with one another. Women and children were taken and sold to the whites, trading them as if they were some kind of commodity. As can be seen, the whites in the area act as the stimulus for these inhumane incursions, for if they did not maintain this detestable traffic in human flesh, the Indians would lose the incentive for their barbarous excursions. (Sabaté in Izaguirre 1925:99)

Note that this was written in 1874 before the rubber boom. The French explorer, Olivier Ordinaire, wrote of his journey in the area:

> At the time of my journey, a "lorenzo" (a specific indigenous group) between eight and ten years of age was worth between 280 and 350 francs; a well formed girl between 300 and 400 francs. Nobody tried to capture the adult men alive as they knew they would escape however far away they were taken, or they would leave themselves to die. The industrialists who organise the correrías and take part in them cannot do without the help of trained Indians for this type of hunting, because alone they would never manage to surprise the savages. When they take possession of the women and children from a dwelling, as a rule they have to kill the father, brothers and husband, in order to avoid any future dispute over the ownership of them, and then set fire to the empty hut...so that they have less sorrow leaving it (1988:98).

He continues by explaining how the kidnapped children were integrated:

> The little savages which have been taken from the nest are generally well treated by their owners, for their well being is in their own interests. Even in these conditions, more than half die shortly after their capture. How many would survive if they were badly treated? It is customary to call the owner of the house daddy, whether or not he was responsible for the death of the child's own parents, and to call the owner's wife mummy. When they have become quite strong, they are partly freed and sent to join the workers who, spread out in groups throughout the forest, collect rubber. They are then given a machete, an axe, maniok, some hunting and fishing implements, and sometimes even a gun. At the same time, their account is established...they pay with rubber. But they have to

renew their provisions. They are also introduced to rum and gin. However hard they work, they are never able to pay off their debt. Many even give up dreaming about this. If the owner feels like doing a little bit of trade, or is leaving the country, they are sold or, and it amounts to the same thing, their debt is sold. Thus their daddy changes quite often (ibid. 117).

We could go on. Historical literature is full of descriptions of Slave raids, the traffic in Slaves and exceptionally tragic tales of the inhumane suffering which was inflicted upon the indigenous population.

In this growing economy, particularly charismatic patrons also stand out, for example, the very famous "King of Rubber" (Reyna 1942), Carlos Fermín Fitzcarrald. An extremely ruthless patron who ran his rubber regime throughout the entire region of Atalaya where he also controlled all trade. He massacred many hundreds of Toyeri and Araseri in Madre de Dios because they did not want to work for him or permit his rubber tappers to gain access to their territories. Amongst other things, several hamlets were destroyed with machine guns (Gray 1996:225). He became world famous because he was an eccentric but educated dreamer who always dressed in a suit and straw hat, lived a life of luxury in the forest and on his steam ships. The "gentleman" of Ucayali died in a shipwreck on the Urubamba river in 1897. But apart from the genocide, and the fact that he created a myth around himself which some still revere, he also played a special role in the recolonisation of Gran Pajonal and Atalaya. In 1896, the then Peruvian President allocated to the Franciscan, Gabriel Sala, the task of travelling to Gran Pajonal with the aim of studying the possibilities for colonisation and the possibility of establishing a railway from Chanchamayo to Ucayali. Father Sala was taken by boat by Fitzcarraldo up river where he was introduced to the patrons who could help him with his expedition. Farther Sala was left in the Unini-Chicosa area, from where he organised his expedition. Apart from the fact that it took him several months to undertake the journey from Ucayali, through Gran Pajonal and up to Chanchamayo because it was the rainy season, Sala also describes in his report how the local patrons, as Fitzcarraldo's subcontractors, organised correrías from Unini within Gran Pajonal, and how he saw houses completely burnt down and he met small groups of indigenous Slave hunters and their white foremen. (Sala in Izaguirre 481-525). At this time there were many rubber tappers in Ucayali. In his report Sala concluded, amongst other things, that Gran Pajonal was virtually uninhabited, that it would be an excellent area for colonisation and that it would only need 10 armed soldiers to keep the Ashéninka under control! His opinion seems a rather superficial one.

> THE PERUVIAN CORPORATION LTD.   N.º 4620
>
> ### PERENE COLONY
>
> Pampa Whaley, 26 de Febrero de 19 5t
>
> Señor Puentero:
> El señor Severo Taype.-
> tiene autorización para salir de la Colonia del Perené, llevan 1 gallina.-
>
> Atto. y S. S.
>
> R. Cresto
>
> mp. JFC-12-50-167

Permit of absence issued by the Peruvian Corporation (Barclay 1989: 169)

Other patrons were, as already mentioned, Carlos Scharff, who survived Fitzcarraldo and took his place as king of the Ucayali, Urubamba and tributaries, in the area which is today the province of Atalaya, where he exercised his unrestricted regime of terror until he was killed by the Amahuaca in 1908. In spite of their crimes, these rubber barons are still national heroes today. In Ucayali and Atalaya they are set up as the models of civilised behaviour. Their culture was refined, they were educated, they knew how to conduct themselves and were forceful. Pianos and velvet furniture. Thus the lines of conduct and rapport with the indigenous population in Atalaya were defined and sanctioned by "public opinion" for many years.

With the collapse of the rubber economy as a consequence of outcompeting on the world market, around 1915 the Ucayali patrons found themselves obliged to search for other sources of income. They now established haciendas where previously there had been rubber collecting stations and where the work force was concentrated. They had shifting periods of success with different products which followed the usual boom and bust cycles. For example, the cotton period; until the mid 1920s this was a very profitable business. Cocoa and coffee also had their moments (and still do). Of the special productive niches, barbasco (Lonchocarpus nicou) can be mentioned, which is also used by the Indians as a poison in fishing. An organic insecticide named Rotenone can be obtained from barbasco. The production of Rotenone boomed throughout the Upper Amazon in Peru and Ecuador until the introduction of the synthetic DDT which took over around the time of the Second World War. But until then, the so called "barbasquerías" were an excellent business. The new products were produced, as before, with indentured indigenous labour. One particular product which was constantly developed throughout this period is tropical hard wood, which is today the most important business for the Ucayali patrons. This extractivist production is today concentrated in the province of Atalaya.

There was drastic growth in the population after the economy became sedentary. In 1928 Atalaya achieved the status of independent district and the same year it was decided to establish a new Franciscan mission. One of the big patrons of the area, Francisco Vargas, who had worked in Scharff's rubber empire, gave lands from his hacienda known as La Colonia, which was situated a little up river from the growing colony of Atalaya, and in general supported the mission in its initial phase with labour and food. In 1932 the Franciscan mission of Atalaya was inaugurated. It must be explained that Vargas and other patrons fully identified with the work of the mission and vice versa, and thus mutually legitimising each other. The introduction of barbasco production on the estates was, for example, promoted by Father Arellano. This old alliance between the Catholic church and the local patrons explains why the idiosyncratic pattern in Atalaya has been able to continue and sustain themselves right up to 1988. After the establishment of the mission, things sped up and people began to move into the Atalaya area. Firstly, the mission built a bridle trail from Puerto Ocopa to Oventeni, continuing to Atalaya along the Unini river. It was built in the 1940s by the Ashéninka of Gran Pajonal and Puerto Ocopa in the lower Perené. It was an enormous task, all carried out by hand. The road was finished ion1946 but was completely destroyed by an earthquake shortly afterwards. But in 1946, air traffic was increasing and the same year the Atalaya landing strip was opened which became the new life-line of the town (Ortiz 1974: 606-651). The "Republic of Atalaya" was still a reality.

VI. The Third Stage
The Consolidation of Indigenous Territory

1. The Land Titling Project

a. Getting help
During the course of the autumn of 1987 and spring of 1988 there was a great deal of communication in both directions between Denmark and

AIDESEP in Lima, regarding the possible formulation of a land titling project. In relation to the participation in the third General Assembly of COICA[44] in Bolivia, in May 1988, there was time to stop over in Lima where the project proposal was discussed in detail and the possibilities with the then president of AIDESEP, Evaristo Nugkuag. There were good technical and strategic experiences from Gran Pajonal which could be replicated and adapted to the situation in Ucayali. Similarly, it was decided that the project should be so comprehensive that in principle it could solve the land issue once and for all in the department of Ucayali, although priority should be given to the province of Atalaya, where the problems were most urgent and acute. The rest would have to follow later. But one thing was that AIDESEP were in agreement with itself regarding how to demarcate the indigenous communities. In actual fact it was the State which formally owned the lands to be divided amongst the native communities and, naturally, only the Peruvian State could issue land titles. In these matters the State was, and is, represented by the Ministry of Agriculture. Thus it was essential for the realisation of a project such as this that the Ministry of Agriculture would agree at a high level to participate by cooperating in a concrete project with indigenous organisations and their technicians. This was a prior requirement for the realisation of such a radical project. At this time there was a positive and open attitude in Lima with regard to the idea of the project, as long as the financial means to achieve the project could be found from international sources. AIDESEP then concluded a framework agreement with the Ministry of Agriculture in Lima regarding the realisation of a land titling project for the native communities of Ucayali, an historical agreement which has had more importance for the democratic development of the Peruvian Amazon than anybody dreamed at the time.

Thus the foundations were laid for the construction of the project. The next step was to find the necessary international economic and political support. It was an appropriate moment in history for positive international relations with Peru. The Peruvian national economy was in ruins. Social violence and political terror were already spreading virtually throughout the whole country and the State was under a great deal of pressure from the different guerrilla movements and their allies in the cocaine industry. The Peruvian government had unilaterally imposed a moratorium on the payment of the State's foreign debt, and had introduced severe restrictions on imports. Production and exports fell catastrophically. The International Monetary Fund (IMF) and international creditors had closed the till and put a hold on all projects being implemented. Technical staff, both foreign and Peruvian, who were working in internationally funded development projects were brutally assassinated by Sendero Luminoso and Peruvian public officials of all sectors were on the look out. The State was to be subdued. Most of the foreign aid agencies and NGOs responded by shutting down their activities and withdrawing completely from Peru. And here we were with a new project which, a) was focussed on one of the most controversial issues: land rights; b) required new international participation, c) worked closely with official Peruvian institutions; and d) was to be carried out in a area where the security situation was, to say the least, questionable.

At first it appeared that all odds were against the project. But there were also advantages to beginning a new project at this time. The Peruvian State, official institutions and employees were in favour of the idea and wanted to maintain possible international cooperation in a situation in which all the international agencies turned their back to Peru. Furthermore, there was virtually no funding for the institutions, many public employees had been made redundant or pensioned off, and there was no funding for projects. This made the project relatively attractive, although there was a great deal of scepticism with regard to working alongside the natives.

It was firstly decided to try to get the Danish International Aid Agency, DANIDA, to support the project. But the fact is that Danish international aid is prioritised and determined according to criteria which broadly divide the funds between multilateral aid, bilateral aid and NGO projects. This latter received a total of around 10% of the total funds. Furthermore, countries, themes and sectors were prioritised. And Peru was not one of their cooperant countries. The only way in which this project could be considered was as an NGO project. But this meant it had to be channelled through a Danish NGO which would be responsible for the use of funds and the project's realisation. Danish aid was not channelled directly to private foreign organisations in non-cooperant countries and this is how AIDESEP would be defined. The most obvious NGO with its base in Denmark which could take on this difficult role was IWGIA, but at this time the organisation had no experience of such complicated indigenous development projects. Nevertheless, IWGIA took on the task and presented the project to DANIDA. DANIDA was rather taken aback by the magnitude, place and context of the project, which was hardly a traditional one at this time within established "development circles". But in praise of the staff of that organisation, it has to be said that they were also very open in respect to new initiatives. They were positive regarding the only possibility which existed to influence the democratic development in a marginal area of the tropical rain forest, to support a group of marginal and stigmatised people and as far as possible to create the basis for a future strategy of sustainable development. Land titling itself was not at that time considered "development" as such, but it was considered as a prior condition for the same (personal communication with DANIDA 1993). The project was approved by DANIDA in 1989. It was an historic moment which marked the beginning of a much wider acceptance of projects with indigenous peoples as a special category of development.

b. Project implementation

The project thus commenced in 1989, setting up in Pucallpa and Atalaya, from where the field work was carried out. It would be rather simplistic to state that there were no problems. The commencement was symbolically marked by the fact that the building complex of the Ministry of Agriculture in Pucallpa, where AIDESEP had use of a small office, were burnt to the ground by unknown terrorists. That was how we knew what we were up against. Nevertheless, the two indigenous implementing agencies, OIRA and AIDESEP, carried out the project. They set up a team of technicians, field staff and coordinators which for the following three years worked surveying, registering and demarcating more than 120 native communities. It was an extremely complicated, difficult and conflict ridden task. They had to manoeuvre with extreme caution in a zone where the Colombian drugs mafia, Sendero Luminoso, the MRTA, three different counter-insurgency groups, hostile patrons, logging companies, new settlers, officials and bureaucrats against the project and political parties were all trying to establish the order of the day. Furthermore, successive Peruvian governments were implementing a series of radical administrative reforms. Thus a policy of decentralisation was implemented which involved the establishment of regional governments with greater administrative autonomy, but without the necessary economic and legislative support from the central government in Lima. Later things were centralised once more, without eliminating the regional governments. The result was a virtual total lack of continuity in the authorities' administration, including many changes of officials and management staff. As opposed to many similar land demarcation and legalisation projects in neighbouring countries, for example, Brazil, Colombia and Ecuador, the Ucayali project was not characterised by the "identity politics" and the inflated rhetoric which often accompanies this strategy. The project team chose a practical and pragmatic approach and in general maintained a low profile, in order to avoid a destructive politicisation of the project. They worked their way from community to community and solved problems as they arose along the way. We will not go into all the more legal and technical aspects of this process as they are considered in detail in other contributions to this book. Nevertheless, there are two methodological characteristics which must be emphasised:

The same indigenous organisations were in charge of the management of the project and the day to day implementation. This was of determining importance for gaining experience, for better or for worse, which was necessary if organisations of this type were to play a real and independent role in the democratisation process within their own developing country. Thus a branch of the Danish organisation responsible for the project was not set up in Peru, with Danish staff to slap the wrist of its "little brother". In contrast, IWGIA chose to supervise the project through frequent monitoring visits, but not through a permanent presence in the project. In development jargon this strategy is called "recurrent intervention". It has many advantages. Firstly, it lets the implementing counterpart solve its internal and external problems itself. It leads to greater responsibility in the long run. It prevents the development of paternalistic attitudes on the part of the foreign sponsor, and at the same time prevents the implementing agency from passing on responsibility for errors to the funding agency. It is also of particular importance in projects with indigenous people that it should be they themselves who negotiate directly with the authorities and other representatives of national society. In the long term this creates respect and a levelling which are otherwise difficult to achieve in a society characterised by racism and discrimination against ethnic groups. The presence of a western European representative in such negotiations would only confirm this ethnic stigmatisation. Although there are of course also disadvantages to not being present throughout the development of the project, it is clear with hindsight that the advantages far outweighed the disadvantages.

The first stage of the large project was carried out between 1989 and 1993 and continued with a follow up project from 1993 to 1995, which also included the beginning of the establishment of seven Reservas Comunales, including separate zones for small as yet uncontacted indigenous groups. In 1996 a third phase started to adjust and bring up to date the geo-referentiation of the boundaries with modern GPS technology. Furthermore, a series of requests for the enlargement of existing communities had emerged and there are always gaps to be filled in. Gran Pajonal was once again incorporated in this latest follow up, through OAGP. The three phases were funded by DANIDA. The supervising and implementing organisations were the same. The project has succeeded in demarcating 162 communal territories, of which 89 obtained new titles and 76 are enlargements of lands already titled (cf. Ñaco Rosas et al. 1997). The demarcation team tried to co-border neighbouring communities, thus creating large blocks of continuous indigenous territories, restoring a total territory of approximately 1.5 million hectares in the Ucayali and Urubamba river basins. This does not include the communal territories of Gran Pajonal, nor the Reservas Comunales mentioned.

The effects of the project have been profound. Indeed, it has changed the entire power structure in the region. Hundreds of former peons left their patrons to join together and form new communities. Now they were landowners and becoming a real political force in themselves, which altered their bargaining position in relation to the regional administration accordingly. A new social reality was taking shape in the former Republic of Atalaya. But it had not been an easy gain.

2. Defending Territorial Integrity

a. The threat to Gran Pajonal

In the late 1980's Peru was propelled into a deep social crises in all sectors of society, giving rise to the Shining Path and MRTA guerrilla movements, as well as illegal coca production for the Columbian drug mafia was spreading all over. Both subversive organizations were based on a modernist developmentalist ideology, nearly identical to the colonist's visions of progress, with absolutely no room for indigenous special interests or politics. The two guerrillas soon got entangled with the native population and their organizations, and increasing conflict arose (cf. Benavides 1992, 1993; Hvalkof 1994a, 1994b). In the areas surrounding Gran Pajonal particularly the Shining Path got foothold through forced recruitment and deadly terror against the native communities. They contacted the Ashéninka dirigente Miguel Camaiteri in order to secure his support for their movement, which he vehemently rejected (personal communication 1996). The rejection of cooperating put the indigenous leadership in Gran Pajonal at odds with the Sendero, who put a price on the head of Camaiteri. The first incursion by a group of still unidentified guerrillas in Gran Pajonal took place in late 1989, where Oventeni was looted, big cattle holders and merchants publicly humiliated, and the OAGP's radio stolen. The subversive commando searched for the Indian leaders too, who fortunately were not present. The incident caused great alarm, the Peruvian army and special counterinsurgency units began planning for declaring the whole area of Gran Pajonal for "zona roja", emergency zone. This signifies that all civil rights will be suspended. In practice it would imply that the Ashéninka would have to leave the zone. The indigenous leadership knew that this would mean the end of the Ashéninka of the Pajonal as they had nowhere to go. Several Ashéninka assemblies were called and the seriousness of the situation discussed. One of the issues was the infiltration by both movements among the settlers in Oventeni, and how to deal with that.

A few weeks after the episode in Gran Pajonal, another similar incident took place among the neighboring Asháninka in the Pichis valley. The president from their regional organization ANAP, Sr. Alejandro Calderón, a very charismatic and dynamic dirigente (who by the way also was a Seventh-Day Adventist) got abducted on December 8, 1989 and later executed by the MRTA guerrilla. The reason for this was his possible involvement in the arrest which led to the execution of another MIR guerrilla leader Maximo Velando back in the winter of 1965/66.

This caused a fierce uprising among the Asháninka in this zone, who in a short time organized a militia and took over the control with the entire Pichis valley. The Ashéninka of Gran Pajonal got inspired by this action and decided to take over the control with Gran Pajonal before the military entered. One early January morning 1990, hundreds of Ashéninka armed with shotguns and bows and arrows, occupied Oventeni and declared it under the control of the Ashéninka Army. They issued a statement giving all supporters, members and sympathizers with the SL and MRTA guerrillas 24 hours free-conduct to leave the zone. A veritable airlift was organized and small planes for two days flew people out.

b. The Obayeriite

The Ashéninka had taken control and the situation was tense. The OAGP had to reorganise. They declared the establishment of the Ashéninka Army a fact, set up an entire defence and surveillance system in the periphery of Gran Pajonal and appointed Miguel Camaiteri as commander-in-headman of the army. All the communities were quite enthusiastically involved. The next step was to convince the Peruvian army that their new Ashéninka militia was able to control the area and obtain arms and ammunition. It turned out to be very difficult to convince the army not to intervene and even more difficult to get any arms at all. After intense diplomacy, their militia gained recognition by the army and no emergency was declared. With their usual Ashéninka skill of backing all horses, they succeeded in obtaining a stock of shotguns and cartridges from different sources.

The commander-in-chief of the militia began coordinating actions with neighbouring groups and helped to organise a similar militia amongst their fellow Asháninka of OIRA in the Upper Ucayali and Lower Urubamba. They named their new coordinated militia system "Ovayeriite", the plural form of Ovayeri, the term which only a few years previously had invariably had a negative connotation synonymous with "criminal" - the ones who performed Slave raids or "correrías" for the patrons. It is interesting to note how an Ashéninka institution can overnight redefine and adapt itself to a new reality when it is needed. This extraordinary ability for ad hoc redefinition of the significance and value of Ashéninka concepts and institutions according to the requirements of a changing social reality is indicative

The Summer Institute of Linguistics has troughout the project rendered valuable logistic support through affordable flights

of the dynamic of Asháninka society. The guerrillas never returned to Gran Pajonal, nor did they succeed in reestablishing themselves in the Ucayali and Atalaya area. By 1995, the numbers of guerrillas had shrunk and they had withdrawn to isolated pockets outside of Ashéninka territory.

c. Civil society

In both Atalaya and Gran Pajonal, the indigenous organisations had grown in strength considerably as a result of the whole process of territorial demarcation which had brought about a degree of organisation never before witnessed. The indigenous dirigentes of both organisations were clear that to be in a position to defend their territorial integrity in the long term and ensure an overall development which took into account the special indigenous needs and survival of their culture, they would be obliged to try to take hold of political power, that is, to participate in the civil democratic process for resolution under the premises of national society. As a result of the social mobilisation and organisational consolidation that was generated, the indigenous organisations arranged for all community members to be registered to vote, and at the following elections in 1995 they ran for mayor and councillors posts at provincial and district levels with their own list which was separate from those of the established political parties. This new indigenous movement, called MIAP (Movimiento Indígena de la Amazonía Peruana) [45] had a national coverage, and took everyone by surprise and won four posts as mayor as well as numerous other positions and other posts in different places throughout the Peruvian Amazon, including overall political control of the provincial capital, the town of Atalaya.

And Gran Pajonal followed suit. Increasing numbers of poor colonists and persons of mixed background from Oventeni now supported and cooperated with the Ashéninka, to such an extent that they managed to elect civil authorities in Oventeni which had a positive attitude to indigenous organisation and even an Ashéninka mayor, although he was an immigrant school teacher. As they achieved the enlargement of the legalised territories, they themselves managed to ensure that the majority of the adult population were registered as voters. Thus they became a factor of formal power in regional politics and in 1996, for the first time in history, they managed to elect an Ashéninka from Gran Pajonal as mayor of Oventeni. In fact it was their leader of many years, Miguel Camaiteri. With regard to Gran Pajonal, it was of determining importance that the elected indigenous authorities in Oventeni insisted that the politico-administrative limits be respected, that is to say, they continued to administrate from the province of Atalaya in Ucayali where they had always belonged, geopolitically, and where there existed a much greater understanding of the culture and indigenous society of the Amazon than that of the choice of the cattle farmers, the colony of Satipo, which was administered from the Andean highland. The response of the colonist society of Oventeni to this insistency was a total boycott of all public initiatives (which came from Atalaya and Pucallpa) such as, for example, health, education and infrastructure.

Many of the patrons are still there, both in Oventeni and Atalaya, but there influence is significantly weakened and discussions now turn around the sort of future the indigenous people will make for themselves and what the economic alternatives to the patron-peon relationship may be.

In October 1996, the London based Anti-Slavery International (ASI) honoured the Regional Indigenous Organisation of Atalaya

(OIRA) with their Anti-Slavery Award. Two of the dirigentes from OIRA, the president and new vice-mayor of Atalaya, Sr. Bernardo Silva and councillor and community organiser, Sr. Milton Silva, were invited to London to receive the award. The ASI is the modern continuation of the "Anti-Slavery and Aborigines Protection Society" which actively lobbied for British intervention to stop the atrocities of rubber extraction in the Congo and Peru at the beginning of this century (Cf. Gray 1990, 1997). The ASI gave the 1996 award to OIRA for "its work in freeing thousands of Asháninka, an indigenous people from the Peruvian Amazon, from debt bondage".

It is an almost surreal experience to arrive in the municipality of Atalaya today and see the town hall and the mayor's office full of industrious Ashéninka who no more than ten years ago were not even registered as Peruvian citizens and did not dare to wear a cushma in Atalaya for fear of the mockery of colonist society, and who were considered no more than a work force commodity. If democracy consists of active participation in politics and decision making by the whole population in order to create common tools to deal with differences and conflictive interests, this has been achieved in this part of the Peruvian Amazon.

V. The Democratic Surplus

Through the process of territorial demarcation and titling, the former patron tied indigenous population of the Ucayali found out that they had certain rights and that there was a society outside of the Atalaya province which would enforce such rights. They learned that it was not necessarily the natural order of things to be owned by a patron, and that they could find allies among other native people. They were excited when things in fact worked out in favour of the native communities and immediately wanted more: their own politicians, schools, a health system and a new indigenous economy. The interest and enthusiasm of the communities, even in the most remote areas, has been impressive. They are currently developing their own bilingual intercultural education system, redirecting the bilingual education introduced decades ago by the Protestant missionaries of the Summer Institute of Linguistics[46]. The latest of the new ventures to be launched is an alternative indigenous health programme involving local shamans, healers, midwives and other indigenous medical specialists in integrated teams with nurses trained in western medical practices, and representatives from the local indigenous organisation. The programme covers 75 indigenous communities in three provinces of the Ucayali region[47]. The project has been a tremendous success, not only in terms of health improvements, but also as an instrument of consolidation of social indigenous mobilisation, participation and self-confidence.

However, the apparent success of the indigenous territorial reorganisation in Ucayali is not the simple result of indigenous ingenuity, self-sufficiency or new ethnic nationalism. It is the outcome of unique conjunctures in the ongoing process of globalization, including:
- the coincidence of a series of global discourses favouring indigenous self-determination in the Amazon, such as the discussions on human rights, sustainable development, bio-diversity, democracy, participation and privatisation.
    - the increasing internationalisation of decision making on normative issues as well as in economics and politics.
    - the explosive growth in communications and communication technology.
    - the privatisation of conventional international development and massive transfers of funds to the NGO sphere.

This new postmodern development has made it possible for local indigenous organisations, through new direct alliances with both national and foreign organisations and NGOs, to reduce or circumvent the influence and significance of local power hierarchies such as that of the former patron regime in Atalaya. There is even a growing tendency to overrule normative decisions of the nation state. It is obvious, however, that these new international alliances also pave the way for new systems of co-optation, which in general can be seen by the growing NGO influence in social and popular movements. However it is imperative for the process that the goal of indigenous self-determination, not as a new "Republic of Atalaya", but as a State-guaranteed endogenous development in a multi-ethnic Peruvian society, is kept in mind and constantly considered when new strategies and policies are drafted by international development organisations who support such "post-development" processes. The Ucayali experience has shown this to be possible.

The highly dynamic and participatory process of titling indigenous territories in Ucayali, as previously described, has itself become a hitherto non-existent field of social interaction. Land titling has become a means of trans-cultural communication - between indigenous society and colonist society and between indigenous society and State/public administration, creating binding social relationships between the parties involved, redefining the position of indigenous society in regional development. The process constitutes a non-ideologized sphere of cross-sectoral and inter-cultural communication. In this field of open values, indigenous rights are pragmatically expressed in specific actions related to common aspects of everyday rural Amazonian life. This new space of social interaction has had a significant impact on the peaceful development of a more democratic civil society throughout the entire area. The process of identifying, demarcating and titling indigenous territories has been imperative for the construction of an indigenous future defining a new role and identity for indigenous society within the national political process. Paradoxically, these "stateless societies", to quote a famous colleague (Clastres 1972), have been the most enthusiastic promoters of regulated civil society. They have been the ones who have introduced the concept of democracy and liberated themselves, and not the society presumably founded on the rule of law which they defend.

Bibliography

AIDESEP (Asociación Interetnica de Desarrollo de la Selva Peruana)
1988a 'Informe Provisional Sobre la Problemática de la Zona de Influencia de la Ciudad de Atalaya Elaborado a Requerimiento de la Comisión de Alto Nivel Creada por Resolucion Ministerial No. 0083-88-PCM'. MS. Lima, Perú.
1988b Informe de Infracciones Forestales Recopiladas en Atalaya y Presentadas ante la Dirección General de Forestal y Fauna, AIDESEP, Lima, Perú.
1991a "Esclavitud indígena en la región de Atalaya" in Amazonía Indígena, Nos. 17

y 18, Año 11, pp.3-14, Lima, Perú. Same as AIDESEP Report 1988a. Edited version.
1991b "Aprovecha mi poco conocimiento de las leyes..." in Amazonía Indígena, Nos. 17 y 18, Año 11, pp. 14-16, Lima, Perú.
1991c "Nos dicen que somos indios y si nos matan nada pasa." in Amazonía Indígena, Nos. 17 y 18, Año 11, pp. 16-21, Lima, Perú.

Amich, José - 1988(1975)   Historia de las Misiones de Convento de Santa Rosa de Ocopa. Ed. Julián Heras. CETA: Iquitos, Perú.

Barclay, Frederica - 1989 La Colonia del Perené. Capital inglés y economía cafetalera en la configuración de la región de Chanchamayo, CETA, Iquitos

Benavides, Margarita -
  1992   "Asháninka Self Defence in the Central Forest Region."
          IWGIA Newsleter 2/92, April-June, pp. 36-45. IWGIA:Copenhagen.
  1993   "Los Asháninka, víctimas de la violencia y la guerra"
          Ideele 59-50, Dic 93, pp. 116-118. Lima

Bodley, John H -
  1971   Campa Socio-Economic Adaptation. Ph.D. Dissertation, University of Oregon.
  1972   Tribal Survival in the Amazon: The Campa Case. IWGIA Document 5. IWGIA, Copenhagen.
  1973   "Deferred Exchange among the Campa Indians" , Anthropos 67 , Freiburg

Brown, Michael F. and Eduardo Fernández - 1991 War of Shadows. The Struggle for Utopia in the Peruvian Amazon. University of California Press:Berkeley.

Bullon Paucar, Alejandro - 1976 Él nos amaba. La Aventura Misionera de Stahl entre los Campas. N/a, Lima.

Casement, Sir Roger - 1912 British Bluebook. Correspondence Respecting the Treatment of British Colonial Subjects and Native Indians Employed in the Collectin of Rubber in the Putumayo District. Presented to both Houses of Parliament by command of His Majesty, July 1912.

Castro Arenas, M. - 1973 La Rebelión de Juan Santos, Editorial Milla Batres, Lima, Perú.

Clastres, Pierre - 1977 Society Against the State, Basil Blackwell, Oxford. (© 1974 La Société contre l'état, Les Éditions de Minuit)

Colono Equis - 1985 "Gringo Roter Instiga a Nativos contra Colonos de Oventenil", El Vigía, Febrero-Marzo, Satipo.

Denevan, William and M.S. Chrostowski - 1970   The Biogeography of a Savanna Landscape. The Gran Pajonal of Eastern Peru. McGill University: Montreal. 69pp.

Document 1 - 1971 Declaration of Barbados. For the liberation of the Indians. IWGIA Document 1. IWGIA, Copenhagen.

Dostal, Walter (ed.) - 1971 The Situation of the Indian in South America. Contributions to the Study of Inter-ethnic Conflict in the non-Andean regions of South America. World Council of Churches: Geneva

Fernández, Eduardo - 1986 Para que nuestra historie no se pierda: testimonios de los Asháninca y Nomatsiguenga sobre la colonización de la región Satipo-Pangoa. Centro de Investigación y Promoción Amazónica (CIPA), Lima

Gow, Peter - 1991 Of mixed blood. Kinship and History in Peruvian Amazonia. Oxford University Press, New York

Gray, Andrew
  1990   The Putumayo Atrocities Revisited. Paper presented at Oxford University seminar on State, Boundaries and Indians. Manuscript.
  1996   The Arakmbut. Mythology, Spirituality and History in an Amazonian Community. Berghahn Books, Oxford.
  1997   "Peru. Freedom and Territory: Slavery in the Peruvian Amazon", in

Enslaved Peoples in the 1990s. Indigenous Peoples, Debt Bondage and Human Rights. Chapter Eight, pp. 183-215. Anti-Slavery International & IWGIA Doc. No. 83, Copenhagen.

Gray, Andrew and Søren Hvalkof

1990a Supervision Report on Land titling Project, Peruvian Amazon: Inscription and Titling of Native Communities in the Ucayali Department, Report to IWGIA, Copenhagen, Denmark.

1990b "Indigenous Land Titling in the Peruvian Amazon' In: IWGIA Yearbook 1989, pp. 230-243. IWGIA: Copenhagen.

Hardenburg, Walter E. - 1913 The Putumayo. The Devil's Paradise. Travels in the Peruvian Amazon Region and an Account of the Atrocities Committed upon the Indians therein. T. Fisher Unwin, London & Leipsic.

Hastrup, Kirsten and Peter Elsass - 1990 "Anthropological Advocacy: A Contradiction i Terms?" Current Anthropology, vol. 31, No. 3, June, pp. 301-311.

Hvalkof, Søren

1986a Urgent Report on the Situation og the Ashéninka (Campa) Population of Gran Pajonal, Central Peruvian Amazon. 50 p. Research Report, Danish International Development Agency and Danish Social Science Research Council, Copenhagen.

1986b "El Drama Actual del Gran Pajonal. Primer parte: Recursos, Historia, Población y Producción Ashéninka". In Amazonía Indigena, Boletin de Análisis año 6 , no. 12. Copal, Lima

1987a "El Drama Actual del Gran Pajonal, Segunda parte: Colonización y Violencia" In Amazonia Indigena, Boletin de Analisis año 7, no. 13. Copal, Lima.

1987b "Proyecto de Etno-desarrollo - Gran Pajonal". 20 p. Chicosa, Setiembre 1987. In: Summary Report, Appendix 3., Danish Council for Development Research, DANIDA, May 1994.

1989 'The Nature of Development: Native and Settlers views in Gran Pajonal, Peruvian Amazon'. In Folk Vol. 31. Danish Ethnographic Society, Copenhagen.

1990 "Roller i Udviklingens Spil: Et eksempel fra Peruansk Amazonas". In: Den Ny Verden nr. 1/90: Udviklingstemaer II. Center for Development Research, Copenhagen.

1994a Summary Report. On field research project: "The Culture of Development and the Amazon Frontier 1985-1987 & Derived Projects and Activities 1987-94. 4 vol. incl. 6 appendices. Danish Council for Development Research, Danida, Copenhagen.

1994b "The Asháninka Disaster and Struggle - The forgotten war in the Peruvian Amazon." In Indigenous Affairs No. 2/94. IWGIA, Copenhagen

1994c "Territorial organization and democracy in Peruvian Amazon. The current Asháninka struggle for land, autonomy and recognition." Paper presented at symposium Ant. 14: 'Sacred Land, Threatened Territories - Contested Landscapes in Native South America' - 48th International Congress of Americanists(ICA), Stockholm/Uppsala, July 4-9, 1994.

1997 "From Curaca to President...Indigenous leadership in Peruvian Amazon: The Ashéninka case". Paper presented at the session: "Contemporary indigenous leadership in the Amazon" AAA's 96th Annual Meeting, Nov. 19-23, 1997, Washington D.C.

1998a "Post-development, Lumber Business and Democracy: The Case of the Upper Amazon in Peru". Paper prepared for the session: Political Ecology and Action Research i Forest Communities. 14th ICAES, July 26 - August 1, 1998. The

College of Williams and Mary, Williamsburg, Virginia, USA
1998b "Outrage in Rubber and Oil. Extractivism, indigenous peoples and justice in the Upper Amazon" in Peoples, Plants and Justice: Resource Extraction and Conservation in Tropical Developing Countries. By Charles Zerner (ed.). Rainforest Alliance, Colombia University Press, NYC. In press. Forthcoming 1998.

Hvalkof, Søren og Peter Aaby - 1981 Is God an American. An anthropological perspective on the missionary work of the Summer Institute of Linguistics. 192 pp. IWGIA Doc. 43. Copenhagen/London: IWGIA/Survival International.

Hvalkof, Søren and Hanne Veber - 1998 "Los Ashéninka de Gran Pajonal". Forthcoming monograph in: Guía Etnografica de la Alta Amazonia, vol. III. Fernando Santos & Federica Barclay (eds.), Smithsonian Tropical Research Institute, Panama

IIP (Instituto Indigenista Peruana) - 1989 'Informe Final Sobre las Medidas Referentes a los Derechos, al Bienestar y al Desarrollo de las Etnias nativas de la Zona de Atalaya.' Documento elaborado por el Equipo Tecnico nominado por la Comision Multisectorial conformada por la Resolucion Ministerial No. 083-88-PCM. Instituto Indigenista Peruano: Lima.

Izaguirre (O.F.M.), P. Bernardino - 1922-27 Historia de las Misiones Franciscanas y narración de los progresos de la geografía en el Oriente del Perú. Relatos originales y producciones en lenguas indigenas de varios misioneros. Talleres Tipográficos de la Penitenciaría, Lima

Kuczynski-Godard, Max - 1939 La Colonia del Perené. Observaciones Higiénicas. Contribución al estudio de la colonización de la selva Peruana. Universidad de San Marcos, Lima.

Lehnertz, Jay F. - 1972 "Juan Santos primitive rebel on the campa frontier (1742-52)" in Actas del XXXIX Congreso Internacional de Americanistas, Vol. 4, Lima.

Malleux, Jorge
1986 "Foresteria" Section on forestry in Gran Geografía del Perú. Naturaleza y Hombre, Vol. VI, chapters I-X, pp. 185-331, Manfer - Juan Mejía Baca, Lima, Perú.

Metraux, Alfred - 1942 "A Quechua Messiah in Eastern Peru", American Anthropologist, n.s., Vol. XLIV, pp. 721-725.

Narby, Jeremy - 1989 Vision of Land: The Ashaninca and Resource Development in the Pichis Valley in the Peruvian Central Jungle. Ph.D. Dissertation, Stanford University, California.

Ñaco Rosa, Guillermo. et al. -1997"Sira Communal Reserve, Introduction", in From Principle to Practice: Indigenous Peoples and Biodiversity Conservation in Latin America. Proceedings of the Pucallpa conference. Iwgia Doc No. 87. IWGIA, Copenhagen.

Ortiz, Dionisio
1961 Reseña historia de la montaña del Pangoa. Gran Pajonal y Satipo. Imprenta Editorial "San Antonio", Lima.
1974 El Pachitea y El Alto Ucayali. Visión histórica de dos improtantes regiones de la selva Peruana. Tomos I-II. Imprenta Editorial "San Antonio", Lima.

Payne, David L. - 1991 "A Classification of Maipuran (Arawakan) Languages Based on Shared Lexical Retentions" in Derbyshire & Pullum (eds.) Handbook of Amazonian Languages, Vol. 3. Part II: Maipuran (Arawakan) Classification. Mouton de Gruyter: Berlin.

Renard-Casevitz, France-Marie - 1980 "Contrast beween Amerindian and Colonist Land Use in the Southern Peruvian Amazon" in F. Barbira-Scazzocchio (ed.) Land, People and Planning in Contemporary Amazonia. Cambridge

University Centre of Latin American Studies, Cambridge, UK.

Reyna, Ernesto - 1942 Fitzcarrald. el Rey del Caucho, Barrantes, Lima.

Sala, Fray Gabriel A. P. - 1897 Apuntes de Viaje de R.P. Fray Gabriel Sala, exploración de los rios Pichis, Pachitea y Alto Ucayali, y de la Región del Gran Pajonal, in Larrabure y Correa, C. (ed.) 1905, Collección de leyes, decretos, resoluciones y otros documentos oficiales referente al Departemento de Loreto, Vol. XII, pp. 7-154. Lima, Perú.

Salazar, Ernesto - 1977 An Indian Federation in Lowland Ecuador. IWGIA Document 28. IWGIA, Copenhagen.

San Ramon, Jesus Victor - 1975 Perfiles Históricos de la Amazonía Peruana. Ediciones Paulinas, Publicaciones CETA, Lima, Perú.

Santos Granero, Fernando
  1987 "Epidemias y sublevaciones en el desarrollo demográfico de las misiones Amuesha del Cerro de la Sal, siglo XVIII", Historica, Vol. XI (1), Pondificia Universidad Católica del Perú, Lima.
  1992 Etnohistoria de la alta amazonía. Del siglo XV al XVIII, Editorial Abya-Yala, Quito.

Santos Granero, Fernando and Frederica Barcley Rey de Castro - 1995 Ordenes y desórdenes en la Selva Central. Historia y economía de un espacio regional. IEP/IFEA/FLACSO-ECUADOR, Lima, Perú.

Schäfer, Manfred - 1988 Ayompari, Amigos und die Peitsche. Die Verflechtung der ökonomische Tauschbeziehungen der Ashéninka in der Gesellschaft des Gran Pajonal/Ostperu. Doctoral dissertation. Ludwig-Maximilians-Universität zu München. Selbstverlag: Amorbach.

Scott, Geoffrey A.J. - 1979 Grassland Development in the Gran Pajonal of Eastern Peru. A study of soil-vegetation nutrient systems. Hawaii Monographs in Geography, No.

Smith, Richard Chase - 1982 'The Dialectics of Domination in Peru: native communities and the myth of the vast Amazonian emptiness.' Cultural Survival Occasional Paper 8. Cultural Survival: Cambridge, Massachusetts.

Stoll, David - 1982 ¿Pescadores de hombres o fundadores de imperio? El Instituto Lingüístico de Verano en América Latina. DESCO, Lima.

Taussig, Michael
  1984 "Culture of Terror-Space of Death. Roger Casement's Putumayo report and the Excplanation of Torture." Comparative Studies in Society and History 26 (3). July University of Chicago.
  1985 Shamanism, Colonialism and the Wild Man: A study of Terror and Healing. University of Chicago Press, Chicago & London

US Department of State - 1913 Slavery in Peru. Message from the president of the United States. Transmitting report of the secretary of state, with accompanying papers, concerning the alleged existence of slavery in Peru. February 7, 1913. 62D, 3rd Session. House of Representatives. Document No. 1366, Washington D.C.

Valcárcel, Carlos A. (juez) - 1915 El proceso del Putumayo y Sus Secretos Inauditos. Imprenta "Comercial" de Horacio La Rosa & Co., Lima

Varese, Stefano
  1973 La Sal de los Cerros: Una Aproximación al Mundo Campa", Retablo de Papel Ediciones, Lima, Perú. (© 1968)
  1982 "Restoring multiplicity: Indianities and the civilizing project in Latin America". Latin American Perspectives, vol. 9, no. 2.

Vargas Llosa, Mario - 1975 La Casa Verde. Seix Barral, Barcelona.
Veber, Hanne M.
    1991a "Schools for the Ashéninka. Ethno-Development in the Making. Paper presented to the 47th International Congress of Americanists. New Orleans, July 7-11.
    1991b "Hvordan Gud kom til Ashaninka. Adventistmissionen i peruansk Amazonas. Tidssskriftet Antrpologi Nr. 23. Antropologforeningen i Danmark, København.
    1992   "Why Indians wear Clothes: Managing Identity across an Ethnic Boundary" Etnos 57 (1-2), Stockholm.
    1996   "External Inducement and Non-Westernizzation in the Uses of the Ahéninka Cushma" Journal of Material Culture, Vol.1, Juli 1996. pp. 155-183, Sage, London.
    1998   "The Salt of the Montaña. Interpreting indigenous activism in the rain forest". Cultural Anthropology No. 13 (3). Forthcoming August 1998.
Zarzar, Alonso - 1989 'Apo Capac Huayna Jesus Sacramento'. Mito, utopía y milenarismo en el pensamiento de Juan Santos Atahualpa. CAAAP: Lima

Notes

1. The term 'Piro' is the most common name for this indigenous group in ethnographic and historical literature. Nevertheless, as Amazonian indigenous groups have become politically organised this has resulted in a political discourse on identity, and this was substituted by the name which these people call themselves by: 'Yíne'. I this article both Piro and Yine will be used as referential terms according to the historical context.
2. Campa was, until the 1980s, the common name generally used for Asháninka, Ashéninka and Nomatsiguenga groups, and sometimes also the Matstiguenga and Yanesha. All these groups belong to the pre-Andean Arawak linguistic family. Nevertheless, Yanesha membership is questionable and they are now generally classified as a separate family (Cf. Payne 1991:354-490, Wise 19). Apart from this main language, they are subdivided into a number of regional dialect groups. The term Campa does not exist in their language, but since the 18th century it has been the preferred term of reference. Today each one is known by its own name, of which the largest group, the Asháninka, is probably the widest known. Since the antiquated term 'Campa' is now practically out of use, weighed down with negative connotations, there is no generic term in use for this body of groups. I have thus chosen to use the terms Asháninka, Ashéninka and Campa according to the specific regional and historic context of the text.
3. It was set up on the former property of the famous rubber patron, Francisco Vargas, on the banks of the Urubamba river. Vargas was the first true landowner in Atalaya after the rubber "boom". He owned several haciendas and farms along both the Ucayali and Urubamba rivers, populated with hundreds of enslaved indigenous peons. He was also the owner of the land on which Atalaya is situated today. (See historical section).
4. Atalaya recently became an independent province in June 1992 through decentralising reforms. Previously, the zone belonged to the province of Coronel Portillo in the department of Loreto; for the sake of simplicity, we have used

the province of Atalaya as the reference zone, although it did not exist either technically or administratively until then.
5. My first field studies amongst the Ashéninka covered three months of the summer of 1975 and were divided into two visits to the region. It was part of a ten month study trip to Peru, where I also studied the national context of the Velasco government's agrarian reform programme. Apart from my visits to the Amazonian region, which also covered other zones and issues, I visited a large number of nationalised cooperatives and businesses on the coast and in the mountains in order to obtain an overall view of the structure and effect of the reform.
6. This comes from the Ashéninka word ovamagaantsi: to kill.
7. From the hotel's guest book (it was the only acceptable hotel at that time) it emerged that nearly all the guests were Peruvian travelling salesmen, with the exception of an anthropologist by the name of André-Marcel d'Ans, who had been there a couple of days before my arrival. This Franco-Belgian colleague later published (1982) an excellent book on the Peruvian Amazon seen from an cultural-ecological, ethno-historical and political perspective. The work provides a detailed description of the political development of the Atalaya region in recent times. D'Ans was employed within the UN-system as, probably, the first development anthropologist specialised in ethnic groups, to contribute to development planning for the zone.
8. It is clear that constitutional legislation existed which envisaged the right of the Native Communities to land, but in practice it had only been used to distribute very small collective areas of land to these communities. The whole procedure and practical interpretation of the public administration of this legislation, including the concept of "community", was a complete reflection of the legislation for peasant communities and of the economy, production form and social organisation of Andean peasant societies. This andino-centrism has characterised the relationship of the Peruvian State, and of society in general, with Amazonian society and has been the cause of innumerable misunderstandings and failed planning.
9. The Shuar Federation, however, did not have a clear policy on the land issue, basically because, since the beginning, the federation had backed cattle raising as the basis for development and legitimisation of their land demands and thus they found themselves ever more a prisoner of their promotion of cattle raising which gradually became a kind of "self-colonisation", since extensive cattle raising in the Amazon demands the continual felling of new areas of forest and the planting of pasture. Thus the federation gradually lost its position as a role model and future indigenous organisations drew up their own strategies.
10. Programme to Combat Racism and the Churches Commission International Affairs of the World Council of Churches.
11. "Symposium on Inter-Ethnic Conflict in South America", Barbados, January 25-30, 1971.
12. The project was largely funded by the Council for Development Research which is the research fund of the Danish international development agency, DANIDA. A small part of the project was funded by the Danish Council for Research into the Social Sciences. The two years of field studies were carried out together with my colleague and wife, the anthropologist Hanne M. Veber and our children. Dr. Veber simultaneously carried out her own research project on the conformation of identity and specific gender issues. It would not

have been possible to carry out the project without the collaboration of Hanne Veber and our children.

13. See: "Petición de varios europeos y criollos para ir a fundar al Pajonal e Informe del Padre Núñez" (Request from various Europeans and Creoles to establish themselves in Pajonal and Padre Núñez's Report) and "Diario de la entrada al Pajonal del Padre Alonso del Espíritu Santo (1735). Pretenden ir a fundar en el Pajonal varios europeos". (Diary of the entry into Pajonal of Padre Alonso of the Holy Spirit (1735). Various Europeans hope to establish themselves in Pajonal". The reports can be found in the Ocopa archives.

14. The place where the first mass meeting was held and where the beginning of the rebellion was coordinated is called Quisopango and is at the head of the Shima mountain stream which links the interior of Gran Pajonal with the river Tambo, with connections the other side towards the mountains through Pangoa and Sonomoro. It is thought that the place where mass meetings were held is situated in the area between the current Ashéninka communities of Pauti and Quirishari.

15. The Peruvian Corporation operated in the zone until 1975, when the Peruvian government nationalised it and finally closed it down. Most of the company's land, which originally belonged to the Asháninka people, had in reality been confiscated without compensation. Nevertheless, the land was not returned to the indigenous communities, but divided into plots and handed over to the company's officials and other employees. Second in line were the peasants and rural workers, and new settlers invaded whatever remained. Only small plots of land were handed out to a few Asháninka communities. The areas of land which the indigenous population received were marginal and so small that it was completely impossible to maintain a subsistence economy on them or to sustain social reproduction any other way. The problem of lack of land is enormous for the growing indigenous population in the Chanchamayo zone of the old Peruvian concessions. Also the high and concentrated level of colonisation of the zone has caused serious erosion and other negative ecological consequences.

16. A number of eye witnesses of the brutal encounter in Mapitzeviari told me how Lobatón and his second-in-command, Jaime Martínez, were taken prisoner and executed on the way to Oventeni. They are still buried there. This is in contradiction with the official version, which is also echoed by Brown and Fernández (1991:239, note 35), who say that Lobatón was taken prisoner and thrown into the forest from an aeroplane.

17. I have in my hands a number of complaints which the Oventeni civil authorities made to the military command at the time.

18. Decree law 20653, Ley de Comunidades Nativas y de Promoción Agropecuaria de las Regiones de Selva y Ceja de Selva. (Law of Native Communities and of Agricultural Promotion for the Forest and Surrounding Regions).

19. Belaúnde had set out his visions for development in his 1959 book with the clever title: La conquista del Perú por los peruanos (The conquest of Peru by the Peruvians.)

20. These large development and colonisation projects in the Selva Central had the common name of "Proyecto Especial Pichis-Palcazu" (PEPP) (Special Project Pichis-Palcazu). In reality this included a series of different projects of different content and with different funders and policies. The project which affected Gran Pajonal most directly was the PEPP Satipo-Chanchamayo Programme, funded by the World Bank. Other projects were: the Palcazu Pro-

gramme, funded by USAID, the Pichis Programme, funded by the Interamerican Development Bank (IDB), the Oxapampa Programme of the German international development agency, and Pachitea-Von Humbolt, under the responsibility of the Swiss and Belgian governments.
21. For a critique of the institutional role of the SIL see Aaby and Hvalkof 1981 and Stoll 1982 . In the interests of truth it must be said retrospectively that the overall effect attributed to these missions was not what happened in Gran Pajonal or Atalaya. In general, criticism, which was justified, did not take sufficiently into account the individual differences which existed between the missionaries in particular, as people, and nor the fact that the missionary organisations were dynamic entities in constant transformation, dogmatic or not.
22. The procedure for surveying, registering, demarcating and titling the native communities in Peru is described in another part of this book (see Gray pp.174-184). In reality, there were already two communities entered in the public registries, Pauti and Tiaventeni, but they were never demarcated.
23. The research project began in April 1985. When I arrived in Oventeni there was a German anthropologist, Manfred Schäfer, there with his wife. He had carried out field work around the traditional Ashéninka exchange systems and economic relations in general. Schäfer published his doctoral thesis in 1988, based on this work which contained a wealth of interviews documenting the exploitation and oppression which colonist society exerted over the indigenous population (Schäfer 1988).
24. The request for demarcation or titling of indigenous communities was not an unknown phenomenon in these international development circles: in the Palcazu and Pichis valleys the PEPP's colonisation plans, which were launched in the early 1980s, aroused severe criticism on the part of the indigenous organisations in the valleys, as well as the NGOs and individuals who were working with the indigenous population of the zone. The projects were rightly criticised for their complete discrimination against the indigenous populations, neglecting their existence, their needs and their rights (cf. Smith 1982; Narby 1989). The persistent complaints forced the funding agency, the Interamerican Development Bank (IDB) and USAID to require that their Peruvian counterparts in the Special Project, before commencing large scale programmes of colonisation, should at least demarcate and title the indigenous community lands that were lacking legal recognition. The technical quality of the demarcation work is questionable, and the areas titled were mostly far too small and on poor soils, but they did constitute a land base, a legal territory for the Asháninka of the valley, on which they could consolidate and strengthen their organisation and eventually expand their legal territory.
25. Organización Ashéninka del Gran Pajonal (the Ashéninka Organisation of Gran Pajonal). In the same year, OAGP became a member of AIDESEP. Today OAGP has 34 member communities.
26. Various officials, topographers and technicians of the PEPP and of the Ministry of Agriculture in Lima made great efforts to support the Ashéninka people throughout this process. Although it is impossible to name them all, mention must be made of Sra. Magda Camargo, of the Ministry of Agriculture, and the now deceased Ing. Carlos Borda, of the PEPP, for their extraordinary effort, solidarity and enthusiasm, without which the Gran Pajonal demarcation project would not have been able to proceed.

27. Witchcraft and accusations of witchcraft are, as in so many parts of the world, an important instrument of social control and power. It is in no way limited to indigenous society but also widespread in mestizo society and amongst the patrons of European origin. Similarly, shamanism and herbal medicine are widespread both in indigenous and non-indigenous society. The context and the ritualisation are, however, different. With respect to the use of the spiritual hallucinogenic, ayahuasca (Banisteriopsis sp.), in the Atalaya zone it is far more widespread amongst mestizo society than the Ashéninka, whose shamanism is much closer linked to the use of tobacco, and where ayahuasca ("kamarampi" in Ashéninka) is mainly used by shamans on special occasions.
28. "Chuncho" is the pejorative name given to the indigenous of the Campa group, which was commonly used by the colonists and patrons throughout the Selva Central and Upper Ucayali.
29. In Peru the term "zona roja" or "red zone" is normally used for special zones which have been placed under a status of military emergency. This means that the army, marines and special forces of the paramilitary anti-subversive corps - counter-insurgency forces (reporting to the Ministry of the Interior) "the Sinchis", previously "the Rangers" - are posted to the zone with unlimited legal powers. All civil rights are suspended, and in actual fact it means that all civilians living in the zone are considered as potential enemies and may be arrested, tortured or killed without any legal procedures taking place. On this occasion, the term "zona roja" was being used only to identify the area with the illegal production of coca and cocaine and what follows from that.
30. Ayacucho is a large provincial capital in the Peruvian mountains. It was established very early during the Spanish conquest of the 15th century. The University of Huamanga in Ayacucho was where SL - Sendero Luminoso (Shining Path) was born in the 1970s and from where it organised its armed struggle in the 1980s. With its Maoist orientation and Pol Pot type strategy it appealed greatly to the politically frustrated youth of the small rural villages, including school teachers.
31. The Movimiento Revolucionario Tupac Amaru - MRTA (The Tupac Amaru Revolutionary Movement). The other guerrilla movement operating in Peru. Its ideology followed a more socialist tradition of the traditional left and clearly had more links with the middle class youth from the cities than Sendero Luminoso. The MRTA had its roots in the MIR guerrilla of 1965/66 and partly in a fraction of the populist party of the left, APRA, of the same period. APRA was at that time in government in Peru, under the leadership of the young president, Alán García Pérez. APRA also had its own terrorist body "Comando Rodrigo Franco" with clear corporativist and fascist tendencies.
32. Central Ashéninka de Río Tambo (The Ashéninka Office of the Río Tambo). A strong organisation which was completely destroyed during the period 1988-94 by Sendero Luminoso through assassinations, kidnappings and terror in its member communities. Río Tambo is, together with Ene and Pangoa, one of the zones which was most affected by the conflict between the army and the SL-drugs traffickers link. CART is now reorganising and fully functioning once again.
33. What the Ministry of Agriculture in Satipo had to do with this nexus is not clear. The contractors and local logging companies in Satipo nevertheless obtained large lumber concessions in 1988, and operated with impunity in the conflict zone which was controlled by Sendero Luminoso.
34. J.B.V. alias "Manquishu" died a few years ago. So did Rufino Valles - of TB.
35. I had a series of interviews with people who maintained that it was no legend,

that the "pishtacos" existed and claimed they had worked for "pishtacos", drawing and quartering the bodies for the sale of fat and other body parts. I also personally have several "strange" experiences in this respect. There are enough coincidences in these stories to justify a real study. But the thought is too perverted and macabre.

36. One meeting was held on the premises of Save the Children in Lima, which had voluntarily put their rooms at our disposal, and the second and final one was held in the offices of the small Peruvian NGO, Vecinos Perú (Peru Neighbours), also in Lima. Save the Children had had a health project in the native communities of Río Tambo and Upper Ucayali for some years. They had their base in the native community of Otica, in Río Tambo, and local offices in Atalaya. Vecinos Perú was an autonomous Peruvian NGO born out of the Protestant international aid agency, World Neighbours. At that time they were funding small projects with indigenous communities in Gran Pajonal and Urubamba.

37. The then president of AIDESEP, Evaristo Nungkuag, an Asháninka from the management team, Segundo Macuyama, and the organisation's legal advisor, Pedro García Hierro - who has also been involved in this publication - participated in the meeting on behalf of AIDESEP.

38. The proposal for the establishment of this Reserve in the Sira area was presented by the very active SIL missionary and communal sympathiser from Gran Pajonal, Richard Rutter. He also attached a map which covered a "tongue" of mountain crests which separated Gran Pajonal from Ucayali and extended as far as the Unini river to the east. The Asháninka organisation, CECONSEC (Central de Comunidades Nativas de la Selva Central - Office of the Native Communities of the Selva Central) which was working in the Chanchamayo-Perené area also discussed a similar proposal that same year. Their interest was due, amongst other things, to the fact that they were looking for alternative areas of land because of the desperate land situation in the old area of the Peruvian Corporation, as has already been mentioned.

39. The conditions of exploitation in the Amazon are also described in literary works, although not specifically relating to Ucayali. Mario Vargas Llosa describes, amongst other things, similar patron-peon relationships in "La casa verde" (1975) (The green house), not as a democratic problem in a modern State, but more as a seductive fascination of the fascist aesthetics which were hidden in this reality.

40. I did not ask the Franciscans of Atalaya about this directly, but they are far more a part of the "colonist institution" and furthermore do not live in the countryside but in the centre of "power" where these conditions are not seen apart from the occasional "filtered" glimps. The history of the Catholic organisations, the social position and the symbolic place and physical location make this line of questioning inappropriate, requiring it to be formulated in another way.

41. In general terms, the extractivist enterprise tried to diversify its production. Apart from lumber, which became by far the most important economic activity in the Amazon region (apart from the illegal production of coca), they successfully tried other products for shorter periods, such as the alternative rubber products, "balata" (Manikara Balata, Mimusops bidentata) and "leche caspi" or "chickle" (chewing gum) (Couma macrocarpa), vegetal ivory "tagua", the fruit of the Yarina palm (Phitelephas microcarpa), as well as the cultivation of native plants and production of special products such as "barbasco" (Lonchocarpu nicou), which was used in the production of the organic insecti-

cide Rotenone, a major export item from 1935-1950. As usual, these small booms only lasted a few years, following the typical boom and bust cycles of Amazon extractivism.

42. It is important to mention that in the Peruvian Amazon rubber trees were tapped by cutting the trees, draining them completely and obviously killing the trees. This practice was a result of the ecology of the growth's frequencies and of the specific social relations of extractivist production in Peru (cf Hvalkof 1998a). This pushed "los caucheros" to the most remote corners of the forest to search for new growth, as it was rapidly depleted in the area. Intimate indigenous knowledge was the key to success. On the other hand, rubber extraction in Brazil was, and still is, based on sustainable recurrent tapping techniques, based on the incision of the tree's bark, which enables the trees to regenerate.

43. This figure is based on statistics from the "Dirección General de Forestal y Fauna-Ministerio de Agricultura, Lima" 1981. 1980 was one of the most productive years in the history of lumber extraction in the Peruvian Amazon. Since then there has been no increase in the number of lumber processing plants. The total number of registered saw mills and other wood processing plants (such as plywood production) in Peru exceeds 450. This figure does not include the many micro-enterprises and one- man initiatives operating.

44. COICA, "Coordinadora Indígena de la Cuenca Amázonica" (The Indigenous Coordination of the Amazon Basin). A pan-Amazonian indigenous organisation for the coordination and formulation of common policies for all the national organisations.

45. The OAGP did not initially participate in the indigenous MIAP (Movimiento Indígena de la Amazonía Peruana) list but ran with a mestizo party and did not obtain sufficient votes at the first round. They later regretted this alliance and have now joined MIAP.

46. The national umbrella organisation for the indigenous peoples of the Peruvian Amazon, AIDESEP, runs a bilingual and intercultural teacher training college in Iquitos. It has now been operating for more than 10 years, and has developed a remarkable educational methodology for rural indigenous communities and indigenous teachers' in-service training.

47. The philosophy and principles of the indigenous health programme have been developed by AIDESEP's health secretariat - Programa de Salud Indigena (PSI) - which is an all indigenous initiative. To successfully run such an ambitious and large scale programme, external funding is imperative. The PSI has received funding for this from a Danish trust fund, the Karen Elise Jensen Foundation, which normally sponsors high-tech equipment for hospital research. The implementation has been supervised and reviewed by NORDECO, a Danish consultancy company.

DEMARCATING DEVELOPMENT:
titling indigenous territories in Peru

Andrew Gray

Previously the colonists were our masters and they exploited us. My grandparents and parents were exploited by loggers. We were robbed, cheated and poorly paid. This was in the past. Now it is as if the people have opened their eyes and have an understanding.

Julio Pacayo, Yíne leader from the community of Bufeo Pozo.

By 1988, the indigenous peoples of the Ucayali region of Amazonian Peru had decided that they had suffered enough. They would take their lives into their own hands and put an end to the slavery and invasions of their lands which had plagued them for over a century. As part of a strong national and international campaign, an ambitious proposal was drawn up to demarcate and title all of the indigenous communities in the area which they presented to the Danish government's development agency, DANIDA.

In August, 1989, DANIDA agreed to support the project with over $1,000,000 for the inscription and titling of native communities in the Ucayali Region of the Peruvian Amazon. The project was formulated and implemented by the Inter-ethnic Association for the Development of the Peruvian Amazon (AIDESEP), which represents the indigenous peoples of the Peruvian Amazon in over forty local federations. The International Work Group for Indigenous Affairs (IWGIA) a non-govermental organization with its main office in Denmark, channelled the money and recurrently supervised the project.

In March, 1993, DANIDA approved a continuation of the project into a second phase, to follow up on extention requests and new communities and also to establish indigenous-controlled protected areas in the inter-fluvial and uninhabited areas between their communities. A third phase granted in 1997, also included the zone of Gran Pajonal which needed adjustments to existing demarcations as well as some new titles. The total programme sought to demarcate, extend and remeassure titles for about 200 indigenous communities and prepare the research and documentation for eight indigenous controlled communal reserves throughout the Ucayali region of Amazonian Peru.

This article, gathered from IWGIA's archives on the project, describes its activities and evaluates its results.1 The activities covered four main areas: inscribing unregistered communities so that they are legally recognised; titling these communities and extending the titles of other communities so that the areas reflect the needs of the people and protect them from encroachment; the evaluation and payment of compensation to colonists who live in the areas being titled and who do not wish to be incorporated into the communities; and the creation of territorial and communal reserves in areas used by the indigenous people to protect the environment and provide them with a consistent supply of game and subsistence resources.

The process of titling indigenous communities and reserves in Peru is complicated and expensive. It began with the Ley de las Comunidades Nativas which was drafted in the time of the military government of Juan Velasco Alvarado (1968-1975) and revised into its current form in 1978. Some titling took place through the government organisation SINAMOS (Sistema Nacional de Movilización Social). This lasted until the second government of Francisco Belaunde Terry (1980-1985). He increased the colonisation of the rainforest and froze the titling process. The subsequent government of Alan García (1985-1990), however, expressed a willingness to title native communities but, in the midst of an almost permanent economic crisis, blamed its lack of action on a shortage of funds.

The government of Alberto Fujimori (1990-) has been less enthusiastic about land titling than its predecessor. Indeed, the most difficult aspect of the project has not been the fieldwork or quality of the demarcation, but the recalcitrance of certain Peruvian authorities and arbitrary obstacles imposed by the government. Nevertheless, the project staff have used an approach of quiet diplomacy, backed up by indigenous protest, which has been effective in achieving practically all of the original goals.

Several factors make this project an important initiative for indigenous land rights in the Amazon. Throughout the world indigenous organisations are demanding that they have more control over their own development, and the key role of AIDESEP as the implementing partner for the project in Peru is a clear example of indigenous peoples taking their development into their own hands.

The style of land titling in the Ucayali project differs from previous approaches in terms of its methodology and scope. Whereas the usual method in titling was to look at each community on its own and not take into account the inter-community relations which make up the ethno-linguistic group as a whole, the method in the Ucayali concentrated on a patchwork model of titling whereby community boundaries coincide to form larger indigenous territorial blocks. By including reserves in the second project, it has been possible to link together clusters of communities into fields of influence operating as indigenous territories. In this way it has been possible to combine two basic principles of indigenous rights: self-determination and territorial control.

The Region and its People

The Region of Ucayali was established at the beginning of 1989, carved from the Peruvian Amazonian department of Loreto, as a part of the García government's decentralisation of Peru. Covering over 102,000 sq. km. of rain forest, Ucayali has a population of at least 178,500. The Region is divided into four Provinces (Coronel Portillo, Padre Abad, Atalaya and Purús), which are further sub-divided into Districts. All Peruvian regions contained a regional assembly of elected representatives until they were disbanded in the coup of April 1992 when the current President Fujimori closed down elected bodies. The regional bureaucracy is run on ministerial lines, although ultimate control still emanates from the centre in Lima. In July 1992, Fujimori began to appoint new regional presidents who currently hold considerable influence.

Of the four provinces in the region, Coronel Portillo contains 90 percent of the population, largely due to the presence of the regional capital, Pucallpa, which contains about 100,000 people. Although the indigenous population of the region is estimated at 30,000 people living in 227 communities, there are many more. The majority of indigenous peoples live in the rural areas which are less populated and where, in most districts, they frequently outnumber the non-indigenous colonists.

The area of the project ranges from the mouth of the River Sepahua on the lower Urubamba in the south, to Pucallpa in the north, and from the Gran Pajonal in the west to Breu and the Upper Purus rivers in the east. Officially, the area of the project contains a total of 12,400 indigenous and non-indigenous people.

The indigenous peoples of the area belong to two different language families: Arawak speakers: Asháninka, Yíne (Piro) and Panoan speakers: Shipibo, Amahuaca, Yaminahua, Cashinahua and Sharanahua.

There is a spectrum of cultures and social organisations throughout the titling area. Some people, such as the Yíne (Piro) of the Urubamba live in large nucleated villages. The Asháninka and Amahuaca on the other hand live in scattered settlements on different parts of their territory. A Shipibo community is marked by its long line of houses stretching sometimes for as far as a kilometre along the river bank. All the indigenous people carry out a mixture of hunting, fishing (the Asháninka emphasise the former while the Shipibo the latter), horticulture and small scale cash activities such as logging or cattle raising.

The most powerful exploiters of the area are logging companies, largely dominated by 'patrons' (bosses). They are colonists who are descendants from the first European colonists during and after the rubber boom, and mestizos who entered between the 1930s and 1960s, when also the neighbouring areas of Chanchamayo, Satipo and the Gran Pajonal were colonised. These powerful colonists form a numerically small but powerful political group, occupying and controlling most of the public offices at a regional and provincial level. Their economy is also based on agriculture, cattle raising and commerce. Throughout the titling programme, they have been present behind the scenes, bribing and cajoling the Ministry of Agriculture to delay recognition of indigenous rights.

More recent settlers have migrated from the Andean highlands over the last twenty years. They are aspiring patrons and in the past have tried to exploit native labour through debt relations but usually they lack the economic resources and political means to become like the old colonists. These settlers are in many cases refugees from the unbearable social conditions in the highlands, where they find themselves caught between guerilla subversion and military oppression (Hvalkof & Gray, 1990a).

Two other key influences have exacerbated the exploitation of the indigenous peoples of the area:- the cocaine mafia and the guerilla movements. The main coca producers in the area consisted mainly of the old colonists and their local associates, but coca production in Atalaya decreased considerably in 1991, after poor quality leaves and more effective policing methods caused a fall in production. The drop in the coca price had a direct effect on the other major influence in the project area, - the guerilla movements Movimiento Revolucionario Tupac Amaru (MRTA) and Sendero Luminoso (SL). The MRTA in 1989 controlled Pucallpa and large areas of Padre Abad while Sendero Luminoso was active in and around Atalaya and the lower Urubamba where they were connected with the cocaine trade. Thus as coca production fell, so the guerrillas showed more interest in other areas.

The Ucayali Region at the start of the project could be portrayed as several indigenous peoples seeking their rights to ancestral lands, opposed by the old colonists and their connections in the logging industry. Whereas the cocaine mafia, the guerillas gradually became less problematic during the project, the military on the other hand, were increasingly allied to logging interests, and at certain moments placed obstacles in the way of the local indigenous organisations.

However this was not at the root of the problem facing the indigenous peoples of the Ucayali.

The Problem

> *The form of slavery in the farm near to my community consisted of working daily without payment. The people did not always know what they were owed...When the community worked for the patron he would give only something to exchange, for example a machete or some axes. The people had to clear a field or cut timber. He gave them not salary...The people did not know and could not complain.*
>
> Carlos Vasquez, Asháninka
> leader from the community of Pensilvania

The serious abuses of human rights in the region of the project have been documented in this volume (García pages 15-80) and elsewhere (Gray & Hvalkof 1990, Gray 1997). Since the rubber boom at the turn of the century, the Asháninka, Yíne, Shipibo and other peoples have been enslaved by patrons. Slave markets were reported in Atalaya as recently as 1954 (Renard-Casevitz 1980:249). During the 1980s representatives of AIDESEP and the Danish anthropologist Søren Hvalkof drew attention of the Peruvian authorities to the existence of slavery in the area. Two reports from AIDESEP (1988a & b) alerted the Ministry of Justice and a Multi-Sectoral Commission confirmed the findings (Instituto Indigenista Peruano 1989).

They identified the existence of debt-bondage and servitude throughout the Atalaya region, where in some cases whole communities were bound to patrons, who perpetuated the system by violence and control of identity documents. Workers were paid little or no wages for a twelve hour day. No worker received social benefits while the treatment and health conditions in the farms and ‚captive communities' were appalling. The reports identified abuses of the freedom of movement, physical abuse, land invasions and racial discrimination. The data gathered at the time demonstrates that at least one third of the indigenous communities in the Atalaya region were affected by human rights abuses between 1984 and 1987 (Gray 1997).

Several parallel problems also affected the indigenous peoples of the Ucayali. The first concerned the ‚uncontacted' or more accurately called ‚voluntarily isolated' indigenous peoples of the region. Several areas of the Ucayali are isolated with limited access. These are watersheds between rivers and headwater areas. In these remote places, reports have arisen of the presence of isolated peoples. Although they usually have some direct or indirect contact with other peoples, as well as non-indigenous peoples, they choose to remain isolated from Peruvian society because they are aware of the dangers of contact - usually decimation by disease and immense suffering. Peruvian law allows for territorial reserves to be created for voluntarily isolated indigenous peoples. The area is recognised as a protected area for them until they decide in their time to make contact with Peruvian society and negotiate definitive land rights. The project planned to title several territorial reserves.

Another problem facing the indigenous peoples of the Peruvian Amazon is ensuring that they have sufficient lands for sustainable hunting. Whereas agriculture and gathering can be replenished within the demarcated area, hunting in particular, depends on the protection of large inter-riverine territories where different species can breed without interference. These territories have been recognised and respected by indigenous peoples throughout their history and they have recently become acknowledged by the Peruvian government as ‚communal reserves'. Communal reserves are designed to enable a people to hold an area in trust for the state; they will not commercialise its resources, but agree to utilise its resources for subsistence purposes only. The project planned four communal reserves.

The problems facing the indigenous peoples of the Ucayali stem from a need for territorial recognition. The communities needed to be titled in a manner which reflected their own needs and connected them together as a protection against the uncontrolled colonisation and unsustainable exploitation of the Amazonian rainforest.

The Legal Background

The Ley de las Comunidades Nativas (22175) of 1978 guarantees inalienable rights to indigenous peoples' territories. The law, although by no means perfect, was one of the most progressive in South America. The law originally consisted of the implementing process for recognising three fundamental land protection principles: inalienability, a prohibition on mortgaging lands and a prohibition on superimposing titles in indigenous community lands. The law recognised the area of land according to indigenous peoples' own defined needs and, in spite of weaknesses, has continued to support indigenous territorial control. Although the passing of the Land Law in 1995 has weakened some of its provisions, the procedures for inscription and titling in Peru are still those set out in the Ley de las Comunidades Nativas (No. 22175, 1978) and the Regulation of the same law still organises its application. Since the law was passed in 1978, many indigenous communities have received titles to their lands but the procedure is complicated, expensive and slow. Indeed titling a community involves no less than twenty-six distinct stages.

A. Procedures for Land Titling in Peru

Inscription

1. The community sends an application to the Ministry of Agriculture requesting inscription. Technical personnel visit the community and produce:

2. Population census
3. Socio-economic survey
4. Sketch map of the territory

On the basis of this information the AIDESEP/Ministry staff draw up:

5. An inscription technical report
6. An inscription legal report

This information is then gathered together and they draft:

7. A Directorial Resolution of Community Inscription (DRCI)

8. The DRCI is then signed by the Ministry in Pucallpa

9. Notification of the Directorial Resolution is sent to the community president, the provincial and district councils and the local Ministry of Agriculture (in Atalaya or Pucallpa depending on the Province).

10. A testimonial of „no appeal" to the inscription is then signed and the Resolution is inscribed officially in the National Register of Native Communities by the Pucallpa office.

Demarcation

11. A team of topographers from AIDESEP and the Ministry makes a visual inspection of the community territory consisting of a detailed study not only of the boundaries but also of soil types to aid in the land type classification.

While in the field the team prepare with the community two documents:

12. A Demarcation Act in which the community approves the boundaries and

13. An Act of Conformity where the community agrees on its officers and the continuation of the titling process.

On their return to the office the teams classify the soil into three parts: those suitable for agriculture, those suitable for cattle raising and those which are to remain as forest. Forest lands are officially ceded to the state but can be used by the community. The forest zones are divided into conservation areas (such as river banks) and areas suitable for timber exploitation. The use-right of the forest areas are guaranteed for the community and all other contracts with outsiders are annulled. The map is now drawn clearly with measurements and accompanying technical information. This is produced in a

14. Descriptive Memorial which is sent to the local Agricultural office which prepares a

15. Testimonial from the Department of Agrarian Reform and Rural Settlement and a

16. Testimonial from the Department of Forestry and Fauna.

The main office in Pucallpa then draws up a:

17. Technical Report for approval of the map and a:

18. Legal Report for approval of the map.

19. A draft Directorial Resolution for the approval of the Map is prepared.

20. The Directorial Resolution is then signed in Pucallpa.

21. The approved map has then to be taken to the head of the community, the provincial or district council and the Ministry of Agriculture for Notification. When these bodies have signed the notification document the map is legally binding. It is posted publicly in the local council and the ministry for 30 days to see if there is any appeal. If there is none a:

22. A testimonial of „no appeal" is signed by the Ministry.

23. A report on the classification of lands and

24. A report on the technical-social study are then approved.

25. The approved titles are registered at the regional office in Pucallpa

26. The titles are sent to Lima.

Expansion follows the same procedure after a new census and socio-economic study has been prepared, explaining the new circumstances for expanding community territory.

When titles have passed notification they are legally recognised and no appeal is possible. However the process does not stop here. The final Ministerial Resolution comes from Lima (although between 1989 and the 1992 coup Presidents of each Region had been authorized by the government to sign the final documents).

In Lima the following stages occur:

1. The areas are approved by the National Cartographical Archival Mapping Programme.

2. The soil classification is approved by the General Office of Forestry and Fauna.

3. The information hitherto gathered is formed into a draft Ministerial Resolution which is checked by the legal division and sent to the heads of the Agricultural Ministry for approval.

4. The Resolution is approved by the head of the General Office of Forestry and Fauna for the forest areas on community lands.

5. The Minister signs the title which is sent back to the regional office and inscribed in the Public Registry Office.

The Lima process can take about 18 months.

In all we can differentiate three points where the titles gain increasing legal recognition:

a. The minimum recognition is at the point of Notification (21). At this moment the maps are legally accepted and any opposition has to be made by appeal. (This was the basic aim and indicator of the titling part of the project.)

b. When the titles are passed on to Lima they are finalised and no appeal can be made except through the Minister in Lima.

c. When the titles receive the Ministerial Resolution an appeal can only be made through the President of the Republic.

The higher the level of approval the more expensive and complicated becomes the appeal procedure. Thus the titles become ever more secure. However the point of notification should be seen as the bench mark of the titling procedure.

Communal and territorial reserves

Communal reserves are very different from community titles. The legal definition comes from several sources. The Ley Forestal y de Fauna Silvestre DL 121147 of 1974 mentions in article 60 that the Ministry of Agriculture will establish Communal Reserves to enable local populations to conserve fauna. It should be recognised by a Presidential Resolución Suprema. Further details come from the Reglamento de Conservación de Flora y Fauna Silvestre DS No. 158-77-AG of March 1977. In Chapter II the definition of reserves is the same as above. In Article 122, native communities are targeted as beneficiaries enable them to manage their resources within their traditional territories. There should be no centres of population within the reserves or any forestry or agricultural work.

A territorial reserve is based on provisions in the Law of Native Communities for areas where there are voluntarily isolated indigenous peoples. This is an easier system and is not based on forest analysis. The steps to prepare a reserve are the following:

1. Declaration of the zone as an area of study by a Resolución Jefectural. This is not essential but guarantees official approval of the work.

2. Justificación Prévia consists of the Ministry of Agriculture requesting the Instituto de Recursos Naturales (INRENA), which is responsible for national parks and reserves, to oversee the preparation. In practice AIDESEP and INRENA made a formal agreement so that the reserves could be prepared without too much bureaucratic formalities.

3. Cartographic identification using aerial photographs, satellite images and maps indigenous communities bordering the reserve etc. are gathered. In addition, a study of all previous work on the area is carried out.

4. The field work then begins by contacting indigenous communities around the reserve and confirming their approval of the proposal. From the community meetings the field workers can ascertain a

preliminary boundary for much of the reserves. Investigation of soils, hydrology, climate and forest form the basis of the main map. Sociological, biological and ecological studies all take place at this point for a detailed report with accompanying maps.

5. The study is then prepared in five parts: soil classification, forest classification, fauna, activities of hunting and fishing and anthropological studies demonstrating the traditional use of the area by the local people. (This was the main indicator of success of the project.)

6. The report and maps of each study are then presented to the Regional and National Governments for approval through INRENA.

7. The report and maps of each study are sent to Lima for Ministerial and/or Presidential approval.

The difference between community and reserved lands is that the latter are not to be used for commercialisation purposes. The lands are ultimately state lands which are handed in trust to the indigenous peoples in perpetuity to manage and administer in the interests of their own and nature conservation. No colonists can by definition be in a reserva communal and so compensation does not apply.

Reserves are more difficult to pass than community titles. However they are not impossible. The territorial reserves with voluntarily isolated peoples in them are usually easier to pass as the environmental surveys are not so detailed. The most important and expensive part of communal reserve work is the research, field work and producing the report (often several hundred pages long each). Once these are presented into the system the main part of the work is done. However, the political will to sign the reserve depends on the current trend of the moment.

B. Changes in the Land Law

In 1993, the Peruvian Constitution was changed so that the value of land and resources was no longer based on productive utility or social functions but on market value. This means that certain provisions on indigenous lands (recognised since the 1920 and 1933 Constitutions) were weakened (Garcia, 1995) . According to the new Constitution, indigenous territories are no longer unmortgagable (inembargable) and so land can now be taken in lieu of debts. Furthermore indigenous land is no longer inalienable, which means that in certain circumstances indigenous peoples can sell off their territories. In addition property rights can be superimposed on indigenous community rights if they are 'abandoned' - a concept never defined by the government.

On July 14th, 1995, the Peruvian government approved the ‚Ley de la Inversión Privada en el Desarrollo de las Actividades Económicas en las Tierras del Territorio Nacional y de las Comunidades Campesinas y Nativas' (Ley 26505). The speed in which the law was passed and the minimal amount of discussion which took place before its promulgation, demonstrates the haste in which the government wanted to re-organise land-holdings in the country. It was promulgated in response to demands by the International Monetary Fund to privatise the agricultural sector. The passing of the law contravened ILO Convention 169 to which Peru is a ratified party.

The new Land Law puts the constitutional changes into practice by opening up all government land for sale. The law covers the coast, highlands and rainforest. The rainforest is being opened up for exploitation - wood, oil and minerals were already available by state concession, but this law now opens state land to anyone willing to pay. If two-thirds of an Amazonian indigenous community vote in favour, their lands can be sold. The effect will be to attract those interested in biotechnology who can buy up large areas at a cheap price to collect samples or utilise recent ‚boom' crops such as uña del gato (Unvaria tomentosa) which raised $40 million in 1994.

These legal changes caused much concern within the titling programme. Although the land law does not take away any indigenous land, it threatens those communities which have titles. However, with information and training, no community need lose any lands providing that they avoid getting into debt and avoid any temptation to sell their lands. They also need to ensure that the existing legislation which applies to indigenous peoples is used and recognised by the authorities - particularly ILO Convention 169 which holds a higher legal priority than the Land Law. The only aspects of the Law of Native Communities (22175) which have been annulled are those concerning buying and selling of land concessions (Articles 11,12,13,17, and 18 in the land section).

The Titling Project

The titling project aimed to liberate the indigenous peoples of the Ucayali from their oppressors. By mapping the communities the AIDESEP wanted to ensure that the indigenous peoples of the Ucayali could gain control of their lands and resources and embark on a process of self-development. This approach was based on one of the main axioms of indigenous rights: self-development for indigenous peoples is impossible without guaranteed territorial rights.

The general objective of the project was the organisation of land titling among indigenous peoples of the Ucayali region and the immediate objectives were the titling of indigenous communities in the Ucayali and the preparation of territorial and communal reserves. These objectives should be placed into the context of land titling as a whole in Peru covering the legal background, the methodology of titling and the procedures.

A: Methodology

> *We prepared the path by the Pajuya opposite to Boca de Yamiyacu and entered there. Meanwhile another group entered over there by Chambiaco, linking with the neighbouring community of Bufeo Pozo. So we have practically joined our land to the patrons and other communities. No one can invade our lands now. We made an agreement with Bufeo Pozo and Unión to link with them. No colonists can enter because of our title.*
>
> Manuel Ergia, leader of the Yíne Community
> of Puija describing community titling

Land titling in Peru has two main approaches which rest on the interpretation of Articles 10 and 11 in the Ley de las Comunidades Nativas. Article 10 says that „The State will defend the property of all the territory of the Native Communities. It will also draw up a map of the community and hand over the property titles." Article 11 discusses the soil classification and argues that all forestry land is „property of the State" which cedes the use of these lands to the community. The result is a contradiction between a principle of inalienability of indigenous lands in Article 10 and a principle State ownership in Article 11. Since the passing of the land law the question of state ownership of forest resources has not been clarified.

Two strategies have been devised to deal with this discrepancy:
1. The legally stronger of the two articles is Article 10. Indeed Article 11 was imposed on top of Article 10 in the revision of the Ley de las Comunidades Nativas by President Francisco Morales Bermudez in 1978. The potential contradiction between the two articles means little as the community title as a whole is what is significant. The State never has and would have great difficulty in exercising any potential right to the forestry lands within the community.

2. The second opinion says that according to Article 11, the State does potentially have the right to take away and use any part of a

community's land which is classified as a forest. In order to prevent this, it is important to ensure that as little community land as possible comes under this heading. This means taking great care in the early stages of the titling procedure to ensure that the census and socio-economic study reflect the full extent to which indigenous communities use their land. In this way more land will be provided under the classification of agricultural and grazing lands.

In Peru these two approaches can be taken to extremes. Option one takes a practical view and tries to short cut the process wherever possible. Some of the procedures can be omitted, but if this were the case, there is always the possibility in the future that someone could appeal against the process. Another short cut can be in the field where topographers do not show the boundaries to the community. The effect can be problematic because the community is not involved directly in the titling of its territory, and paths which act as physical boundaries may not correspond to the area on the map.

The problem with option two is that it takes the bureaucratic procedure very literally and considerable time and effort has to be devoted to the socio-economic study. In areas where only a few titles need to be done this is comparatively straight-forward, however in a project seeking to title hundreds of communities, socio-economic studies of fifty pages or more are impossible (Hvalkof & Gray, 1990a).

The style of the Ucayali titling project aimed to avoid these extremes and to combine strict adherence to the legal procedures without expending so much energy on the documentation that the targets could not be met. There were three main principles behind the titling in the project:

1. The largest areas of land possible were included in the titled area. Many areas, particularly those bordering on the Gran Pajonal, are important for indigenous peoples for hunting.

2. Wherever possible, community lands were joined together to make larger territorial areas. The net result was a patchwork of communities forming blocks which act as a great deterrent for colonists wanting to invade.

3. Community participation was fundamental to the process of demarcation. Teams were trained in the community by promoters to prepare the boundaries of the community so that when the topographical teams arrived an area was already defined.

Yine

Cashinahua

B. Compensation

> *Compensation payments have been particularly useful in titling or extending community lands easily and peacefully. If there had been no payment of compensation, there would have been many problems because the Ministry of Agriculture supported the patrons and did not want to give one piece of land more than necessary to the communities.*
>
> Bernardo Silva, President of OIRA

Another problem with the titling process in Peru was what to do with settlers on community lands. According to the Ley de las Comunidades Nativas, settlers who live within community lands have to move out when the titling is completed unless they are invited to be incorporated. In order to be able to leave and establish themselves elsewhere they need compensation (mejoras) for the lands on which they have settled. This has always provided a problem for titling in Peru. The government is expected to offer the compensation in the form of government bonds noted both for their lack of value and rare appearance.

The usual way of dealing with colonists has in the past been to title communities around the settlers leaving strange shapes around the borders of the territory where settlers remain. However this has done nothing to solve problems between settlers and colonists; on the contrary, in most cases it has exacerbated the hostility. For example in the lower Urubamba, SINAMOS (the land titling agency during the time of the Velasco military government when the Ley de Comunidades Nativas was established) titled several communities in the 1970s which avoided the colonists' lands. The result was too small areas for the indigenous communities to survive and the continuing economic dependence on the colonists. The communities thus became islands in a sea of colonists rather than the reverse.

The titling project incorporated the idea of paying cash compensation to settlers who were willing to move from communities receiving titles. By including this social problem within the titling process, a new dimension transformed the project out of its legal domain and into the area of social and cultural development.

C. Organisational Strengthening

> *Our organisation has been working with the communities. We can break this exploitation now. In the past our ancestors did not have an organisation, but now in Atalaya we have OIRA, a regional organisation, in Lima at a national level we have AIDESEP and also interna-*

> *tionally we have COICA which also represents us. I think that in a short while with our capacity for organisation we will not see any more patrons and there will be no more slavery. We will have only ourselves, managing and defending our lives. We will know ourselves the way to lead our own communities.*
>
> Bernardo Silva, President of OIRA

In addition to the titling work, the project invested a percentage of its funds towards strengthening the existing indigenous organisations in the area. AIDESEP received considerable support not only for its administrative work and publishing the results of the project, but also for opening a much needed office in Pucallpa which was the centre of operations for the project. OIRA (the indigenous organisation of the Atalaya region) received a house which became the titling base for fieldwork in the upper Ucayali and Urubamba. In Purus and Yurua the effect of the project was to form the indigenous organisations, Federación de Comunidades Nativas de la Província de Purus (FECONAPP) and in Coronel Portillo the Federación Nativa del Distrito de Panilla.

The organisational element of the project should not be underestimated. In order to explain to a people the law and the rights accruing to a native community, AIDESEP sent out orientation teams to the area. Each potential community learnt how to help the topographers establish their boundaries and were able to explain their problems with colonists. By raising these questions, the project prepared communities for the recognition of their land rights and strengthened their capacity for the defence of their territories.

Structure and Activities of the Project

On May 19th 1988, AIDESEP signed a contract (known as the ‚Convenio') with the Ministry of Agriculture which agreed to inscribe and title the territory of the native communities in Ucayali. The three entities involved were AIDESEP, the Unidad Agraria Departmental XXIII Ucayali (which has its main office in Pucallpa and a subsidiary office in Atalaya) and the Dirección General de Reforma Agrária y Asentamiento Rural, Lima. The Convenio was sealed by a Ministerial Resolution, the highest guarantee possible in the Peruvian bureaucratic system. This provided the legal basis for all the subsequent work which was shared between AIDESEP and the Ministry of Agriculture.

The project operated according to the relationship between the three parties to the Convenio. AIDESEP was responsible for the project and its leadership suffered constant attack from colonists as the company

El Sira Reserve

Ucayali River

bosses and settlers tried to stir up opposition. Throughout the project AIDESEP's political handling of the project was firm and supportive. The leadership constantly emphasised the rights of indigenous peoples according to the law and with the compensation facility in the project, it provided a strong counter to the opposition.

The project contained the largest administration and budget AIDESEP had hitherto handled. The organisation runs on elected leaders from communities, many of whom are not experienced in development work, and from time to time IWGIA provided technical assistance and counselled the leadership to ensure that the administration of the programme went as smoothly as possible. Even so there were some difficulties from time to time.

AIDESEP's close relationship with the local indigenous organisations, such as the Indigenous Organisation of the Region of Atalaya (OIRA) was very important. OIRA provided the basis of the information from the field. The office in Atalaya has become a focal point for indigenous peoples throughout the region and has been the backbone of the project in the upper Ucayali and lower Urubamba. The new organisations in the Purus and Yurua is another result of the project impact.

AIDESEP operated with one inscription team, consisting of social promoter and a motorist who would carry out the census, elaborate the socio-economic study and draw a draft map of the proposed titled area. For demarcation and extension, AIDESEP had two teams consisting of three topographers, one soil classifier and one motorist. They carried out the inspection of the territory and its boundaries, drew up the Demarcation and Approval Acts for the community assemblies, classified the soils and wrote the official reports. For the territorial and communal reserves, AIDESEP had a forestry engineer, an anthropologist, a soil classifier and a cartographer who produced the maps and the reports. In practice, when the demarcation and extension fieldwork was completed, the inscription and titling teams reformulated into two more teams to support the preparation of the reserves.

In the Pucallpa office, AIDESEP employed a coordinator, a technical assistant, a lawyer, two cartographers and two secretaries. Initially all the administration was carried out from AIDESEP, Lima, which received some infrastructural support for this. As the project continued, it became increasingly decentralised and a local administrator in Pucallpa carried out the book-keeping and accounts. The titling programme provided infrastructural support such as computers, office equipment, theodolites and field materials.

The national and local offices of the Ministry of Agriculture were the other parties to the Convenio. The local administration of the Ministry of Agriculture in Pucallpa and Atalaya raised the greatest obstructions to the project. Many of the local level officials were closely connected to the colonists or were themselves settlers from the highlands. When the project began, several functionaries saw indigenous rights as a „threat to civilisation" and an obstacle to national progress and integrity. This attitude permeated to officials in the regional government as well.

There is no doubt that as the project continued, several of the individuals working in Pucallpa began to understand the nature of the work and shifted their position markedly to one in favour of the project. Partly this was because they realised that the project was a positive way of solving many land problems, and partly because it offered job security and experience. However more often than not, those officials who began to favour the project were removed to other tasks.

The central administration of the Ministry of Agriculture in Lima was easier to deal with than the local administrators and officials. Most of the staff have little or no ideological or personal interest in the Ucayali region. The Ministry in Lima was attracted to the project because of the collaboration between Peruvian and foreign institutions. The project took the pressure for titling away from the Ministry yet preserved some prestige for the government.

The Ministry provided four teams, two for inscription, titling and extensions, one for administrative work and one for the reserves. These were covered by the Ministry's costs and co-ordinate with AIDESEP. In practice, the AIDESEP teams were usually accompanied by a member of the Ministry to ensure that both parties were in agreement about the areas demarcated.

The meetings of the Parties to the Convenio punctuated the project every few months in Pucallpa. IWGIA representatives attended these sessions. During these meetings, complaints, opinions and targets were discussed and plans were made for the field work over the subsequent period of the project. Success of the project has much to do with co-operation between the AIDESEP and Ministry staff. The best way to avoid corruption and assure loyalty and interest is to offer good working conditions. The project thus included advantages for the workers, such as social security insurance, holiday bonuses, sufficient equipment in the offices, life insurance for field workers, risk allowances for field workers and seniority bonuses.

Project Activities

These can be divided into demarcation of communities and the establishment of territorial and communal reserves.

Demarcation Activities

1. Fieldwork and mapping of community lands.

2. Notification of title to the community with an approved map. At this point the title is legal and can only be over-ruled by an appeal.

3. Registration of the title at the regional and central offices of the Ministry of Agriculture and final approval by the Minister of Agriculture.

One of the difficulties with the programme was ascertaining the number of communities to be titled. The original totals from the two projects within the programme was about 120, but as people went into the field, requests from more communities appeared and while others could not be completed for a variety of regions. The project clearly aimed to obtain the full recognition by the government for as many titles as possible. The base line of the project was the approval of every map and notification because at this moment the law is in operation. However the third aspect of government approval could not be guaranteed by the project as it involved political will on the part of the government. In spite of this, after much lobbying, all the communities which sought titles did receive their ministerial resolution.

Territorial and Communal Reserve Activities

1. Field work in the reserve areas on a multi-disciplined basis.

2. Production of the multi-sector report and maps. This should be presented to the Regional Government and INRENA in Lima. At this point the Reserve has been ‚received' by the government and begins a long process of recognition.

3. Approval by the regional and central governments and final approval by the President of the Republic.

The basic goal for this project was the presentation of each reserve report to the government. At this point, the work of the reserve is done and should not be questioned. The subsequent stages are political and depend on the climate at the time. A reserve may take several years to be approved.

The Project in Action

Although the project began in February 1989, the funding and first full meeting of the Convenio did not take place until late September. AIDESEP managed to keep the project going through loans and temporary adjustment of the budget. This gave enough time for the Ministry to start the inscription and titling, while formal contractual letters and a detailed budget was drawn up. The initial eight month's work saw 20 communities inscribed and 17 with demarcation resolutions drawn up (Hvalkof & Gray 1990b).

However AIDESEP and Ministry differed markedly in their methodology. The Ministry wanted to limit the size of community titles to appease colonists, while the indigenous peoples wanted recognition of their historical ownership of the area. A solution was found where indigenous claims were treated as the basis for the demarcation while compensation for colonists was built into the programme. However, the colonists mobilised considerably during the last months of 1989 and the leaders of AIDESEP, OIRA and the Asháninka organisation of the Gran Pajonal all came under threat.

A meeting of the Convenio parties in early February 1990 cleared the air and a technical meeting with the Ministry of Agriculture established a series of principles for the titling. The communities were to be reorganised into co-bordering blocks wherever possible and aerial base maps provided to facilitate the cartography. This effectively doubled the titling area. The work was divided into zones made up of blocks of communities.

Unini Zone Blocks: Ramon Castilla, Tsipani, Chicosa, Shahuaya
Atalaya Zone Blocks: Sepa, Inuya, Tahuanti, Mencoriari, Apinihua
Alto Ucayali Zone Blocks: Nueva Italia, Sheshea, Incari, Inuria
The Zone Blocks: Purus, Yurua and Padre Abad were subsequently developed.

However as soon as some problems were resolved, others appeared. During this period disturbances in Atalaya increased. The cattle ranchers had formed an association to oppose the project and the activities of Sendero Luminoso were closing in on the town which was under martial law. Furthermore, the military commander of the area did not support the project. All these factors made the fieldwork difficult and dangerous. A boat from the Ministry was ambushed at one time and AIDESEP teams were threatened (Aparicio & Hvalkof 1990).

Nevertheless, by the end of June, 1990, the intrepid teams had inscribed thirty two communities and demarcated fifty-five. Seventeen maps were sent to the Ministry in Pucallpa for approval but the government kept delaying the signing. It was subsequently discovered that the loggers and other colonists were offering bribes in the region of a thousand dollars or more to prevent these documents being signed (Gray 1990).

On July 28th the government of Alberto Fujimori won the election and proceeded to change completely the orientation of the Garcia government, encouraging resource extraction in the rain forest. Lumber and cattle interests immediately took these as signs of encouragement. At the same time Fujimori carried out several economic reforms to control inflation which had risen to 7,000 per cent in the last weeks of Alan Garcia. The value of the dollar plunged. AIDESEP was thrown into financial disarray. Several projects were collapsing and so from July to September everything was frozen. The result was catastrophic in Atalaya. The co-ordinators could not pay the compensation which had been promised to the colonists moving out of the communities nor had the field workers or Ministry employees received their travel expenses. The resulting discontent among the officials and the colonists was exploited by the lumber patrons who with the military commander tried to halt all further titling. Ucayali's Ministry of Agriculture chief, Gandhi Davila, even called for a public meeting in Atalaya on 23rd October to build up opposition to the project. Fortunately, just before the meeting, AIDESEP had managed to unfreeze its money supply and the colonists and workers received what was owing to them (Hvalkof 1990, Aparicio 1991).

By 1991, thirty-six communities had been inscribed and fifty-nine demarcated. Twenty eight titles were in Lima (two had been sent back to Pucallpa for clarification). In March and April the colonists renewed their opposition to the project, and in spite of the verbal promises of the Ministry of Agriculture in Pucallpa, little progress was made with the signing of the twenty-one communities remaining. The next few months were critical. The project co-ordinators put all their efforts into resolving the problems of compensation and bringing around the personnel from the Ministry. Compensation was worked out for the outstanding cases and meetings were held with the regional government in Pucallpa. Huerto Millar the President of the Region was slowly brought around to the project and the head of Agriculture, Gandhi Davila was replaced by a more neutral person, Carlos Rincon de la Torre.

In AIDESEP also there were changes and in July the Assembly of AIDESEP was held in Iquitos where a new leadership was elected.. During the same month, a team spent nearly a month travelling through the Purus organising and identified the 21 communities ready for inscription and demarcation. This work was undertaken with no opposition from colonists because the region consists almost entirely of indigenous people.

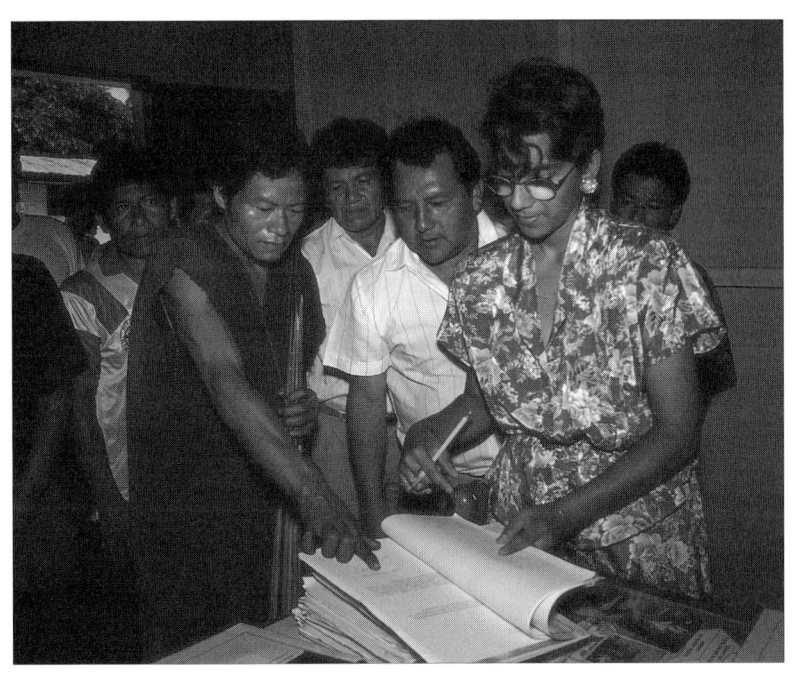

The Convenio meeting in September, 1991 could see that the annual progress of the project had been slow. The inscribed communities had increased from 36 to 44 and demarcated communities from 59 to 62. The meeting consisted of a blunt exchange between the new AIDESEP leadership and the Ministry. The Ministry officials tried once again to slow matters down, but this time, the officials from Lima supported AIDESEP. On the third day of the meeting the Ministry officials in Pucallpa capitulated and agreed to sign the maps of 17 communities from Atalaya. The agreement was televised and the Ministry of Agriculture, Pucallpa promised to complete the work of the project (Gray & Andersen 1991).

Even though this was an improvement, the situation in the project was still critical. Just over half the target had been completed. Yet there was a chance to take advantage of the break-through at the September meeting of the Covenio committee. The money from the first application was due to finish in December, 1991. The question was whether to close the project then or complete the original target by extending it until June 1992. IWGIA and AIDESEP sent an additional application to DANIDA.

AIDESEP sent several teams into the field between October and December. During this period the final communities in Atalaya were checked and demarcated, then the communities in Purus were inscribed and demarcated. Furthermore the work in Yurua was started and a survey of the extensions in Padre Abad were completed. By December 1991 the DANIDA application had been approved and all the fieldwork for the project was completed apart from the demarcation of some of the Yurua communities which was finished in January, 1992.

With the field work completed, the focus of attention was drawn to the Ministry of Agriculture in Pucallpa. During January, 1992, the seventh meeting took place of the Convenio Committee. AIDESEP now had the final statistics of the titling project. The final total of communities to be completed was verified as 114. Thirty two of these consisted of territorial extensions (amplicaciones). With all the demarcation work completed, the onus was now on the office to produce the documentary material ready for signing. Representatives from the Ministry in Lima insisted that if the maps were not signed Ucayali regional staff would be dismissed (Aparicio 1992).

On April 6th, 1992, President Alberto Fujimori unilaterally suspended the Peruvian Constitution and proclaimed rule by Presidential Decree until a new constitution was formed. The immediate measures included the dissolution of the Peruvian Congress and the Judiciary. A consequence of the auto-coup was the dissolution of all regional precidencies and assemblies. All the diputados who attended the previous Convenio meeting in January and the President of the Ucayali Region,

Sr. Huerto Millar, was removed from office. Thanks to the support from Lima, the Ucayali project was, amazingly enough, not affected by the coup as were other projects in the Amazon (Gray 1992).

The AIDESEP team worked from eight in the morning until eight at night for seven days a week from February to April and by then all the final reports and maps were complete. Most of the maps were signed and notifications (this is the moment when the law provisionally takes effect) were presented in Purus, Coronel Portillo and Atalaya. Only Yurua and Padre Abad remained to be notified which subsequently took place. The draughtsmen had drawn over 200 maps and 60 communities' documents had been completed. During June and July 1992 the final work was done on the titles, completing the fieldwork and documentation. The project, against all odds had accomplished its object (IWGIA, 1992). Meanwhile a proposal for a second phase was drawn up by AIDESEP extending the titling programme and working on preparations for the establishment of communal reserves. This was sent to IWGIA and DANIDA and approved in March 1993.

AIDESEP then met with the Ministry of Agriculture in Lima and Pucallpa to plan the time schedule for the signing of the final titles of the first phase, to approve an extension of the Convenio until December 1995 and confirm that a multi-sector commission would look at development prospects in the titled areas. Nevertheless, with a consistent pressure on the government, to comply the Convenio addendum was signed in May, 1993 (Dahl & Gray 1993).

In spite of the delays, three field visits were made in 1993 which inscribed three communities, demarcated nineteen and evaluated seven colonists' lands for compensation. At the end of 1993, the only obstacle facing the project was the negative attitude of the regional Ministry of Agriculture (Gray & Parellada 1993). AIDESEP and IWGIA eventually sent a letter of complaint to the Minister of Agriculture and the Minister of the Presidency (which co-ordinates the operations of different Ministries in relation to non-government organisations). This led to some movement at the beginning of 1994. Negotiations began and an agreement was signed between the Ministry and AIDESEP on January 14th 1994 to approve all the titles pending from the first phase and begin approving maps from the second (Parellada 1994).

However, whereas nearly all of the field work for the community titling had been completed by September, the Ministry of Agriculture had not approved one map.The director had insisted that the Ministry do all the final map drawing and not one had been completed. In the previous phase AIDESEP had completed all the maps and documentation themselves and the Ministry only had to sign them.

Meanwhile AIDESEP began fieldwork on the communal and territorial reserves. The largest reserve, El Sira, was so big that work was divided into four stages covering areas in the regions of Huanuco, Cerro de Pasco, Ucayali and the Pichis. The first three were to be done by AIDESEP and the last, the smallest area, by the Asháninka organisation of the Pichis, ANAP (Apatiuaraka Nampitzi Asháninka Pichis). The Huanuco zone was carried out over a six week period in March and April. As a result of this activity the communities in Puerto Inca formed their own federation, Federación de Comunidades Nativas de Puerto Inca (FECONAPI). The team negotiated an agreement with colonists from the Israelita sect so that all were in favour of the reserve. The report was completed in July. The Cerro de Pasco and Ucayali were carried out later in the year and the beginning of 1995. However, the ANAP side of the work was not so smooth and organisational differences led to a delay.

By the end of 1994, the project suddenly found itself in jeopardy. Although all the fieldwork of the community titling had been finished and about half the Sira reserve, there were several major problems: the Ministry had not yet approved a single map while co-ordination between ANAP and AIDESEP was so bad that the reserve demarcation team had to leave the area. The teams were feeling despondent and morale was at an all time low.

In January 1995, a serious discussion took place to find out whether the project should be closed for the time-being. The Ministry in Lima became concerned with the lack of movement in Pucallpa and as a result of their insistency, Pucallpa began approving the maps. The Asháninka, meanwhile, had held a summit of all their federations, including ANAP, and an agreement was made to support fully AIDESEP's titling work in Sira. This was accompanied by an improvement in staff relations (Gray 1995a).

Once these problems were sorted out the project looked in better health. The compensation had all been paid and the fieldwork for the community titling was complete. Some support was given to the local federations on the advice of the DANIDA evaluation mission and this gave the local organisations the means to provide more support for AIDESEP and the staff of the project (DANIDA 1994).

In March-April fieldwork was carried out in the Upper Purus reserve (for the so-called ‚Mashco-Piro') and the draft report was completed in July. In August the fieldwork for the Ishconahua reserve was carried out. At this time, a group of Murunahuas were reported from the Yurua area. As there was guerilla unrest in the proposed Cashibo reserve it was decided to replace work in the Aguaytia with a visit to the Yurua to demarcate a reserve for the Murunahuas which was carried out in October (Parellada & Andersen 1995).

By May, the Sira reserve work had moved on well. The team completed the final fieldwork in the Ucayali section of Sira in April and prepared the report immediately. Fieldwork for the communal reserve „Inuya-Tahuania" (known previously as „Asháninka") was carried out between July and September 1995 and a few months later, another team was studying the communal reserve „Yurua" (known previously as „Yaminahua"). The communal reserve „Tamaya-Caco" (known previously as „Shipibo-Conibo") was completed in December. One change has been the cancellation of the Yíne Reserve which was to have been created around Sepahua. The team considered the area was too heavily logged to be a feasible prospect because there are over forty different logging companies (Gray 1995 b & c).

One brief titling visit was necessary to check maps of two communities. 18 maps had been signed by May and this rose to 28 by August. Things slowed down until the end of the year because the teams were working on bringing out the reports on the territorial and communal reserves. By the end of 1995, all the fieldwork for the project had been completed and about half of the demarcated community maps had been approved. Reports were ready for the three parts of the Sira reserve, the Upper Purus and the Inuya-Tahuania reserve.

In November, the local elections saw several indigenous representatives voted into municipal office. The two most successful areas were in Yurua and Atalaya where indigenous peoples now control the municipal councils. This took place through the strong election campaign, the registration of voters project supported by IWGIA and the awareness raising which emerged through the whole titling programme.

During 1995, the situation of AIDESEP's main administration became serious. A consortium of donors helped out with the basic costs, while the debts were negotiated with the creditors. The work on the administration meant that the leadership was constrained in its political work. However, the project's administration from Pucallpa functioned well through the year. 1996 was the programme's final of phase two. It saw a reduction in the teams and a concentration on writing reports and pushing the community titles through the map approval stage, ready for notification. The project two main phases were finally completed on 1st of August (Parellada & Andersen 1996, IWGIA 1996).

Evaluation of the Programme

When reading an account of the project, it seems miraculous that AIDESEP managed to achieve so much against so many odds. The main problems stemmed from the logging patrons and their influence on the Ministry of Agriculture in Pucallpa. In addition, guerrilla unrest, problems of AIDESEP's administration and personnel difficulties arose at different times during the eight years of the programme. Indeed there was no moment when the titling work was not encountering some problem or other.

In both phases delays beset the programme and only through AIDESEP's intensive lobbying and actually carrying out the work of the Ministry, was it possible for the project to fulfil its goals. At the end of the first stage, 114 communities had been demarcated with maps approved, while on completion of the second phase, 95 communities were titled, remeasured and colonists were relocated. The team in Pucallpa continued to follow through these last remaining titles and by 1998, all the titles were approved totalling 209 communities covering two and a half million hectares. When the reserves are included the total rises to nearly the double.

By January 1992, 65 colonists had received compensation. Since then approximately 40 more colonists were compensated by the titling project which brings the total to over 100. This covers about half the number of colonists in the area. However, taking into consideration those who left because of guerilla unrest, in total between two-thirds and three quarters of the colonists moved from the area of titling project. Some colonists still remain on plots of land between communities, but they are surrounded by indigenous lands and are not able to expand their influence.

Community Titling

> "Where is the title?" say the colonists. Now we can show them the map!
>
> Javier Prado, Asháninka leader from San Francisco o Tziqueato

The inscription and demarcation were the most time-consuming aspects of the project. This was almost entirely due to the difficulties in lobbying the regional government to comply with the requirements of the Convenio. On the whole, AIDESEP took a quiet approach, but occasionally were able to mobilise local indigenous organisations to make public their discontent with the government's attitude. The constant demands by the Ministry of Agriculture to check the maps does mean, however, that the work was been carried out with considerable accuracy.

The size of the communities on average range between 10,000 and 5,000 hectares, although some communities were as large as 50,000 hectares. In each case the size was determined by the community members and the limiting factors were boundaries with neighbouring communities and the production needs. For example, fishing communities such as the Shipibo stretch out along the large rivers, such as the Ucayali. Their settlements are usually nucleated and they claim less land than the Asháninka communities of the interior. The Asháninka have hunting communities which are dispersed throughout a much larger area and consequently require larger extensions of territory than the Shipibo.

The Ministry of Agriculture regularly tried to find criteria for reducing the amount of land claimed by the communities, but AIDESEP and the technical teams vehemently supported the legal provision recognising indigenous community territories according to their needs. In this way, the Ucayali titling project managed to provide three times the average size of community titling in other parts of Peru (1,500 hectares).

The territorial and communal reserves were the work of the second phase of the project. They were divided into two groups: the first are ‚territorial reserves' or ‚territorial delimitations' which are recognised as a preliminary form of titling for indigenous peoples who have not been contacted. The second are ‚communal reserves' which are hunting areas protected for particular clusters of communities, usually in the headwaters of rivers or streams.

Territorial Reserves

For our future we want to sow our yuca and maize. We want our territory. This is what we want. We want to fish. In the streams we can catch fish. All this we want for ourselves and for our children. Our struggle is the defence of our community against the people who want to screw us up.

Javier Prado, Asháninka leader from San Francisco o Tziqueato

1. Upper Purus Reserve

The fieldwork for the Upper Purus (Mashco reserve) took place in March and April, 1995. The difficulty with this reserve is that whereas the existence of isolated people was clear, there was no positive identification as to who they are. The report (AIDESEP 1996a) contains interviews made with Cashinahua, Sharanahua and colonists. All of these informants called the unknown group ‚Mashcos' which made the team initially conclude that they probably belong to the Harakmbut people of the Madre de Dios. However, the only current use of the term

Mashco is in the hyphenated term for the three women of the Manu National Park who speak a dialect of Piro language and are known as ‚Mashco-Piro'. Of the Panoan groups, the Cashinahua and Sharanahua could not understand the Alto Purus people. It is therefore unlikely that they are Nahuas or Yora who are a nomadic Panoan-speaking people in the southeast Peruvian Amazon.

The descriptions of the Upper Purus people as light-skinned and tall makes some think that they could be the survivors of a highland group who went into the forest or else a group of wandering Tupis who came over from Brazil. Although possible, these options would be remarkable as Quichua or Tupi (Cocama-Cocamilla) groups in the Peruvian rainforest are the most oriented to the national society. Although an Arawak-speaking Culina from the Purus could not understand the ‚Mashcos', several members of this language-family are unintelligible to each other (for example Culina and Piro are unintelligible).

Professionals from the Manu National Park said that people from the Mashco-Piro group (Arawak speakers) had been seen in the Upper Chandless river, close to the area of the territorial reserve. This was confirmed by Ada Castillo, head of the Manu National Park who thinks that the Upper Purus people are a sub-group of Mashco-Piro. As a result of this information, it was decided to call the reserve the ‚Delimitacion Territorial Alto Purus'. The general conclusion is that the group is most probably ‚Mashco-Piro' but as the term Mashco is offensive, recommends that the official term is finalised when the people decide to emerge and identify themselves. The report for the reserve was presented to the Ministry of Agriculture on January, 3rd, 1996 (AIDESEP, op.cit.). The area proposed in the study was 768,848 has. and was approved on April 1th, 1997.

2. The Ishconahua Reserve

This fieldwork was completed in August, 1995. The report provides a detailed account of the visit to the rivers Utuquinia and Calleria. Thirty years ago, the South American Mission brought 20 Ishconahuas from the headwaters of the river Piyuya (an affluent of the Calleria) to the Shipibo community of Calleria on the Ucayali. Now only two of these people are still alive, and they are integrated into the Shipibo community. The team travelled with these two men and went as far as the Yurayacu where the uncontacted Ishconahuas come to collect turtle eggs.

The workers in this area told the team that the Ishconahuas occasionally come to the settlements and take machetes, rifles, salt and sugar. They were able to establish from the Ishconahua guides and the inhabitants of the area that the Ishconahuas live on the Peruvian border with Brazil at the Cerra Sentinela. They are Panoan speakers but do not seem to have any direct contact with the other groups. They live in malocas in the headwaters of the rivers near to the Cerro and cannot swim in the broader streams (one Ishconahua had drowned on the South American Mission expedition).

In June 1995, there was a substantial drop in the price of coca (an arroba was worth $100 and in two months it slumped to $4). This means that the loggers in the area are going further into the interior and could, in the next few years, force the Ishconahuas into their border homeland (Parellada, 1997). The team suggests that AIDESEP looks for strategies as to how to deal with the event of the Ishconahuas or other groups making direct contact with the national society. The report was presented to the Ministry of Agriculture on May, 3rd, 1996 and the recommended area was 294,875 hectares (AIDESEP 1996d). It was finally approved with a extension of 275,665 hectares.

3. The Murunahua Reserve

The original plan was to carry out fieldwork among the ‚uncontacted' Cashibo of Aguaytia by the end of August 1995. Apart from being delayed, there were several problems with this reserve. In the first place there was guerilla unrest in the area and there have been problems with the drug trade. It was suggested that this reserve be delayed until a future phase of the programme to give time for the situation to improve.

Instead, the team which had returned from doing the fieldwork in Yurua on the ‚Reserva Comunal Yaminahua' in October 1995, heard that there was a group of uncontacted Murunahuas which are a subgroup of the Yaminahuas. They carried out the required fieldwork and discovered that the Murunahuas are Panoan-speakers living in the headwaters of the Piquiayu river. The Murunahuas do not want people moving into their territory and they have already shot one Asháninka in the area. There are currently three women from the Summer Institute of Linguistics trying to make contact with them.

The Murunahuas are a Panoan-speaking people who appear during the summer months in the Upper Yurua and Mapuya. They appear to live in communal houses and are thought by indigenous peoples of the region to be semi-nomadic. They live in the headwaters of river during the rainy season and come down during the drier months (March to September) to hunt, fish and gather turtle eggs.

The situation in the area is serious and in September 1995, the logging patron Mario Peso went into the forest and was responsible for shooting a Murunahua in the leg. When he had recovered in two weeks, the loggers told the Murunahua to take them to his people. Two were found and brought back to the loggers' base camp. By December, 1995, 35 Murunahua had been captured by the loggers. The situation is thus extremely dangerous. The report was handed into the Ministry of Agriculture on 30th July, 1996 and the recommended area for the reserve was 481,560 hectares (AIDESEP 1996f). It got finally approved on April 1th, 1997.

Communal Reserves

The 1993 Convenio of Technical Cooperation between the Instituto Nacional de Recursos Naturales (INRENA) and AIDESEP was designed to cover five communal reserves: the Ucayali section of El Sira reserve and one each for the Asháninka, Yaminahua, Shipibo-Conibo and Yíne. Eventually, the El Sira reserve was carried out as a whole covering three sectors of study each involving a reserve report (Arbaiza et al. 1998). The only reserve which could not be carried out was the Yíne reserve which was situated in an area of intense logging. However the extensive work on El Sira compensated for this. The completed reserves are as follows:

1. El Sira

This the largest reserve and in order to accommodate the enormous task, the fieldwork and studies have been divided into three river areas: Pachitea, Pichis and Ucayali. Five separate reports were brought together for the overall ‚Sira' report uniting the three areas. The report is over 400 pages long and combines detailed ethnographic and environmental material gathered in the field with extensive library research (AIDESEP 1996b).

A reserve on the area of the Sira mountain range has been a proposal since 1966 but the idea for a communal reserve arose in 1987. The area of nearly one million hectares covers the Regions of Ucayali and Andres Avelino Caceres. To the north the area starts as a range of hills not far from the confluence of the Pachitea and Ucayali rivers. The reserve is bounded on the west and east sides respectively by the Pichis/Pachitea and Ucayali rivers. To the south the area meets the Gran Pajonal. The peoples who use the area or live on its borders are Yanesha, Asháninka, Cacataibo, Yíne and Shipibo.

The area is largely inaccessible to non-indigenous peoples because of the labyrinth of steep hills and gorge-like rivers which feed the Ucayali. The area is primarily the ancestral territories of the Asháninka who hunt throughout the hills. The lakes in the Sira are considered sacred to the indigenous peoples as entries into the underworld. The hunting territories, sacred sites and the fact that the area is one of the rare pre-Pleistocene refuge areas with high biodiversity, make it a crucial area for conservation.

Unfortunately colonists are beginning to make their way towards the Sira from the Pachitea. The main threats come from gold miners and colonies of the Israelitas religious sect who migrate from the highlands. These threats make the protection of Sira a matter of urgency. The report for the integrated areas of El Sira was presented to INRENA on March 23rd, 1996. The total area is 698,533 hectares.

2. The Reserva Comunal Inuya-Tahuania

The fieldwork for the Reserva Comunal Asháninka was completed at the end of September, 1995 according to plan. From Atalaya the team travelled to all the communities around the proposed reserve. On the Inuya river (an affluent of the Urubamba) they reached Bobinzana and made several visits into the centre of the reserve. Then they visited each community until they reached the Tahuania (an affluent of the Ucayali).

The fieldwork found strong support for the reserve from the communities although they are not entirely Asháninka. Seventeen are Asháninka, one is Yíne, one is Sharanahua and two are mixed Asháninka/Yíne. The Yíne requested that rather than it being called the Reserva Comunal Asháninka, it be called the Reserva Comunal Inuya-Tahuania so that people recognise that it covers the territory of more than one indigenous people.

The main problem in the area arises from loggers. Inuya and Tahuania are both sources of timber, although Mario Peso, the largest wood patron has left the area (moving to the territory of the Murunahua - see above). Most of the indigenous communities work for a patron on the basis of debt bondage. This occurs during the periods when there is no other productive activity available. The Ministry of Agriculture in Atalaya is supportive of the idea of a reserve.

The AIDESEP team considered that the wood concessions are in specific areas upriver from the communities and do not touch the central area between the rivers which should be reserved. Thus it should be possible to demarcate a reserve for over 300,000 hectares without affecting the timber interests. The report was handed into INRENA on May 3rd, 1996 and the proposed area is 370,760 hectares (AIDESEP 1996e).

3. The Reserva Comunal Yurua

The fieldwork for the ‚Yaminahua reserve' in the Yurua was carried out between October and December 1995. The area under study was on the right bank of the Yurua and consisted of five communities: two Yaminahua, two Asháninka and one Amahuaca. The non-Yaminahua communities requested that the reserve be called Reserva Comunal Yurua.

The area consists of low hills and extensive bamboo forest. There are no forestry concessions in the reserve although the military has established a Unidad Militar de Asentimiento Rural outside of the proposed area where they have been unsuccessfully trying to settle colonists on the frontier with Brazil. However, reports show that the Military is actively trying to exploit the wood of the area around the town of Tipishca. None of this is thought to affect the reserve.

The Yurua Reserve will border on the proposed Reserva Territorial Murunahua which was demarcated carefully so as to avoid confusion. The Murunahua reserve will provide a buffer between the Yurua and the Tahuania/Inuya reserves. The report was handed into INRENA on 1st October 1996 with a proposed area of 118,956 hectares (AIDESEP 1996g).

4. The Reserva Comunal Tamaya-Caco

The fieldwork for this reserve took place between October and December, 1995, using the teams which had completed the Yurua and Tahuania/Inuya reserves. This area covers the Shipibo-Conibo communities on the Ucayali downriver from the Inuya-Tahuania backing onto those which had their lands extended by the demarcation work of the project.

The area is important because it contains some lakes of special ecological and spiritual value to the Shipibo. When the teams reached the area, they discovered that an attempt had been made to designate a reserve in the area a few years ago, but the initiative had faltered through lack of funds. The team therefore completed the work and drew up accurate maps. The report was submitted to the Ministry of Agriculture in December, 1996, proposing a reserve comprising 132,120 hectares (AIDESEP 1996c).

The Technical and Political Aspects of the Programme

The technical work carried out by AIDESEP is generally considered to be outstanding. Not only was all the field work completed but all the reports for the reserves were all written up and presented to the Ministry of Agriculture. The Ministry has double checked the fieldwork and is satisfied with its quality and furthermore, people from different parts of Peru have now come to visit the project to learn from its experience. All that remains now is for the Ministry to approve the reserves.

As a participatory project, the programme worked closely with local communities. Each community determined its own area and the technical teams were accompanied by local leaders. If the project were to take place now, GPS systems would probably be used which would enable a greater level of participation, with community members actually carrying out the measurements and drawing up the maps. As it was, in the project, technical teams, consisting of both indigenous and non-indigenous professionals worked closely with local community members, achieving the highest level of participation and control possible with the technology available.

At a national government level, the politics of development took place in a climate of competition between different camps. The „development" camp wanted to exploit the rainforest to raise revenue to pay off Peru's debts. The „conservationist" camp wanted to increase the profile of Peru as progressive in order to attract foreign confidence. The philosophy of the titling and reserve project was consequently designed to steer a balance between the development and conservation factions.

Throughout the period of the project, the Peruvian government has given lip-service to the ‚conservationist' camp while pursuing a stridently developmentalist programme. Signing the addenda to the Convenio in May 1993 took considerable effort and, as in the previous phase, AIDESEP encountered numerous difficulties with the Ministry of Agriculture, Particularly obstreperous was the office in Pucallpa. However, eventually they came round and all the communities were titled. Yet this had meant a massive campaigning work for AIDESEP and the local organisations.

The project can be said to have succeeded in spite of, not because of, the attitude of the government. The pressure on the government came from three areas: the local level: national level and international level. On the local level, communities and local federations worked together so that at critical moments they would travel to Pucallpa and insist on the recognition of their community titles. At the national level, the AIDESEP team worked on the Ministry of Agriculture in Pucallpa, largely through working directly with the employees so that the work was pushed ahead. International support came during the monitoring trips when meetings were arranged between IWGIA and Ministry officials.

Criticisms of the Programme

The titling programme received criticisms from within Peru for two main reasons. One was that it was too large and that the Ministry took advantage of the potential financial advantages to slow the process down. The project was thought to be too expensive. However, a study was made in April 1992 to compare the Ucayali programme with cheaper titling projects elsewhere in Peru. The conclusion was that when the amounts spent on organisational strengthening, compensation to colonists, infrastructural support and size of titled area are considered, the costs turn out to be equivalent.

Another criticism of the project was that a large amount of money passed into AIDESEP's administration and this led to the breakdown of its financial capacity. AIDESEP certainly suffered serious administrative difficulties during the programme and at one stage the organisation was in serious debt from one project. Some of these problems were inherited from the past, whereas others resulted from taking on too many projects at the same time. However, those organisations which carefully monitored and provided AIDESEP with the necessary technical assistance did not encounter problems with their projects (Andersen 1990, 1992). Nevertheless, between 1994 and 1996, at times AIDESEP felt as if it was under siege both from within and outside. The problem with administration therefore did not affect the programme but had severe consequences for the rest of AIDESEP. On the advice of DANIDA, IWGIA played a leading role to trying to solve the broader problem. This took place by keeping the organisation functioning and dealing with the strategies for solving the financial crisis.

Lessons Learnt

Several lessons came out of the experience of working with the land titling programme.

1. Land titling cannot work without the full participation of indigenous peoples, determining the areas they need and accompanying or carrying out the technical work.
2. Although national legislation frequently provides for the recognition of indigenous rights, the implementation can be difficult. Strong indigenous organisations and the capacity to carry out national and international campaigns are important aspects of titling work.

3. Indigenous organisations need to be strengthened to ensure that the titling work is recognised by governments and that they have the capacity to take advantage of the titles to benefit the communities. This involves a holistic approach to development.

4. Indigenous organisations sometimes encounter difficulties when controlling large-scale projects, and technical assistance and monitoring is also useful to aid transparency and accountability.

5. Compensation can be a fruitful element in dealing with colonists, although there can be a problem if negotiations are open-ended as this can lead to inflationary demands.

6. It is possible to create a development partnership with indigenous organisations within an overall principle of self-determination. Furthermore, large-scale projects can take place without the intervening agencies needing to open up offices in the recipient country.

Throughout the indigenous world, invasions of territory have been the most effective way of destroying peoples' cultural identity, subsistence base and their way of life. The Ucayali land titling project has sought to rid the area of abuses and to demonstrate the effectiveness of land titling when controlled by indigenous communities. The aim has been to promote indigenous self-determination which in this case stems from a controlled sustainable economical base, together with a respect for human rights.

Future Work for the Programme

The original discussion of the land-titling project with DANIDA in 1989 was that demarcation provides the basis for development and that after titling is complete, follow-up activities should take place. A series of activities was suggested by AIDESEP.

1. Training and capacitation. This should take place at a community and federation level and consist of a variety of programmes in different areas. Political work and understanding of the laws; economic alternatives; cultural strengthening and territorial defence were the main subjects raised.

2. The communities are keen to know the extent that they can sustainably use those resources which can be used or sold. This applies particularly to community lands. Research into different resource potentials, such as forest inventories and the possibility of managing animals and fish were raised.

3. In this context the notion of ‚Plan Maestro' or Master Plan for the reserves is important. This should consist initially of an indigenous council or committee based on community and federation organisations which would control access to and activities within the communal reserves.

4. The territorial reserves which contain the non-contacted peoples have to be treated with caution. A suggestion made was that strategies be adopted how to react should any of the non-contacted peoples wish to emerge from their territories. Medical support was particularly important and a discussion with the Summer Institute of Linguistics which has dealt with these situations before would be useful.

5. Activities should be carried out to ensure that the communities have enough resources to prevent them returning to their old slave-owning patrons. Some patrons still remain in the Ucayali and the indigenous people of the area have shown signs of going back to them because they need certain basic necessities which can only be bought with cash or labour such as salt, sugar or kerosine. Advice on how and where to sell products is important. Connected to this should be programmes of reforestation and the management of wood on indigenous territories.

Conclusion

For me, the project has been very beneficial because all the communities have had their lands demarcated and soon will be titled. It is important that the communities know the boundaries of their lands and that any outsiders, such as our brothers from the highlands, who migrate into the areas will see the limits beyond which they cannot cross.

Bernardo Silva, President of OIRA

The mobilisation and assertion of indigenous territorial rights in the project have considerably ameliorated the human rights abuses which had been taking place in the Ucayali. The on-going titling process has

caused a major „exodus" from these farms of enslaved or „kept" Asháninka labourers who, encouraged by the land titling project and the legal actions taken by AIDESEP, now claim their freedom and land-rights in the surrounding areas. This sudden drainage of the labour force has put severe pressure on the economy of both the old colonists and the new settlers, which is completely dependent on very cheap or free Indian labour.

What is critical is that the land titling is of a sufficient quality to benefit the indigenous peoples of the region. Quality in land titling refers to the amount of land. Too small areas do not liberate indigenous peoples but squeeze them into locked reserves where they cannot support themselves and are forced to become a labour supply for the local non-indigenous population.

The Convenio (agreement) under which the project was structured between the Ministry of Agriculture in Lima, its regional office in Pucallpa and AIDESEP was broadly successful, although recalcitrance by officials in Pucallpa influenced by colonists has been a problem which has only been overcome by constant monitoring and pressure from AIDESEP. The project has been hard work and has had its stronger and weaker moments. The administration was an important learning experience for AIDESEP and the technical team which has done the fieldwork and documentation for the land titling is now one of the most experienced in Peru.

The frequent visits of IWGIA consultants to Peru was an important element in the model of development used in this project. Whereas AIDESEP, an indigenous organisation, has been responsible for the implementation of the work, IWGIA has closely monitored and advised AIDESEP and OIRA, participating in the Convenio meetings with the staff, the Ministry of Agriculture and formulating joint evaluations with the indigenous organisations. The visits have kept a balance between unnecessary interference and ensuring that the administrative and technical elements of the project are of a high standard.

The visits to the communities demonstrate the great enthusiasm with which the titles have been received. Furthermore the people see their titles as the beginning and not as the end of a development process. Follow-up work is important to prevent the indigenous people in the communities looking once again to patrons to seek financial support. Once they start taking loans the old debt-bondage relations will return.

From the perspective of titling and reserves, the project has, against all odds, succeeded in practically completing all of the land titling in the Ucayali region. Furthermore, the reserves fulfil an important function of linking together the different community blocks. In this way lands titled from the Pichis are linked to the Ucayali by the Sira reserve, while the communities on the Ucayali are connected to the communities of the Yurua by the Inuya-Tahuania and Murunahua reserve; while the lower Ucayali are connected to the Purus by Tamaya-Caco, Ishconahua and the Upper Purus reserves.

The effect of the titling programme can be seen in its repercussions on the indigenous peoples of the Atalaya and Yurua areas. In the November 1995 elections for municipal councils and mayors, both areas became controlled by its indigenous peoples. This has been particularly apparent in Atalaya which has been the area where the programme started in 1989. Now, not only are indigenous peoples regularly visiting the town to trade and meet, but they now control the apparatus of the state. This has occurred because the land titling programme involves constant discussions with AIDESEP about the rights of indigenous peoples and as the titles become recognised and the communities realise their potential, the whole complexion of the area has changed.

Indigenous organisations have also become strengthened through the project. Small amounts of infrastructural support mean that the four Shipibo organisations of the Ucayali are becoming increasingly more effective and new organisations appeared in Purus, Yurua and the Pachitea. A particularly gratifying manifestation of organisational strengthening has come in Atalaya where OIRA has received the Anti-Slavery Award for its titling work in liberating people from slave-like conditions.

During their visit to Europe to receive the Anti-Slavery Award, the president of OIRA explained that when the project started in 1989, the indigenous peoples of Atalaya were in conditions of slavery. Atalaya was a mestizo town, controlled by logging interests. Ten years later, Atalaya is full of indigenous peoples, the Mayor and municipal council are indigenous and communities are free. The Ucayali region is now at a threshold. The conditions of oppression have been received, now the challenge is to continue by establishing a basis for indigenous self-determined development.

> *We want to live quietly. We in our community want to live in peace, drinking our masato. We hunt animals throughout our land. Now we have no problems with colonists. There are no patrons nor colonists, just Asháninka.*
>
> Julio Rios Sintzicama, Head of the community Santaniari

Notes

1. This article makes particular use of the initial analyses of the situation of the area made by Soren Hvalkof (Hvalkof & Gray 1990a), and the final reports of the two phases drafted for IWGIA by the author (IWGIA 1992, 1996). The AIDESEP reports on the reserves were key sources for the descriptions in the evaluation. The statements from indigenous representatives from the area were collected by the author throughout the period of the programme.

References

AIDESEP, 1988a „Informe Provisional Sobre la Problemática de la Zona de Influencia de la Ciudad de Atalaya Elaborado a Requerimiento de la Comisión de Alto Nivel Creada por Resolución Ministerial No. 008388-PCM". MS. Lima.
AIDESEP, 1988b „Informe de Infracciones Forestales Recopiladas en Atalaya y Presentadas ante la Dirección General de Forestal y Fauna". Lima.
AIDESEP, 1996a "Estudio Tecnico de Reconocimiento y Delimitacion Territorial para el Grupo Indígena no contactado de ‚Alto Purús'." Pucallpa
AIDESEP, 1996b "Reserva Comunal ‚El Sira'" (Two Volumes) Pucallpa.
AIDESEP, 1996c "Evaluación Final: Proyecto Titulación de Comunidades Nativas y Reservas Comunales". Pucallpa.
AIDESEP, 1996d "Estudio Técnico de Reconocimiento y Delimitación Territorial del Grupo Etnolinguístico Ishconahua." Pucallpa.
AIDESEP, 1996e "Reserva Comunal Inuya-Tahuania." Pucallpa.
AIDESEP, 1996f "Estudio Técnico de Reconocimiento y Delimitación Territorial del Grupo Etnolinguísitico Murunahua." Pucallpa.
AIDESEP, 1996g "Reserva Comunal Yurua". Pucallpa.
Andersen, K. B., 1990 "Report on the Administration and Accounting of the Peru Project." IWGIA, Copenhagen.
Andersen K.B., 1992 "Administration and Accounting report to IWGIA on the Indigenous Land Titling Project in Ucayali Peru." IWGIA, Copenhagen.
Aparicio T. and S. Hvalkof: 1990 "Second Update Report Land titling in the Peruvian Amazon: The Ucayali Department." IWGIA, Copenhagen.
Aparicio, T., 1991 " Landtitling Project in the Ucayali Region (Peru): Report to Danida on AIDESEP and IWGIA: Mid Term Evaluation of the Project (August 1989-December 1990)." IWGIA, Copenhagen.
Aparicio, T., 1992 "Landtitling Project in the Ucayali Region, update." IWGIA, Copenhagen.
Arbaiza, S., B. Huertas, C. Aguirre, 1998. 'El Sira Communal Reserve' in Gray A., Parellada, A., & H. Newing (eds.) From Principles to Practice: Indigenous Peoples and Biodiversity Conservation in Latin America. IWGIA Document No. 87. Copenhagen.
Dahl, J. & A. Gray, 1993 "Evaluation Report of the DANIDA/IWGIA Titling and Communal Reserve Project in Ucayali Region, Peru." IWGIA, Copenhagen.
DANIDA, 1994. "Titulación de Comunidades Nativas de la Región de Ucayali y el Establecimiento de Reservas Comunales, Perú." Misión de Evaluación. Copenhagen.
Garcia, Hierro, P., 1995. Territorios Indígenas y la Nueva Legislación Agraria en el Perú. Grupo de Trabajo Racimos de Ungarahui, Documento IWGIA 17. Lima. Peru.

Gray, A., 1990 "Report on the Fourth Commitee of the Convenio for the Inscription and Titling of Native Communities of the Ucayali Department, Peru." IWGIA, Copenhagen.

Gray A., 1992 "Evaluation Report to IWGIA on Indigenous Land Titling Project, Ucayali, April-May, 1992." IWGIA, Copenhagen..

Gray, A., 1995a "Report of IWGIA Visit to the Peru Project: ,Titling of Native Communities of the Ucayali Region and the Establishment of Communal Reserves." IWGIA, Copenhagen.

Gray, A., 1995b "Report of the Visit to Peru: The Titling and Communal Reserves Project in Ucayali Region." IWGIA, Copenhagen.

Gray, A., 1995c "Report of IWGIA Trip to Peru." IWGIA, Copenhagen.

Gray, A., & S. Hvalkof, 1990 "Indigenous Land Titling in the Peruvian Amazon." in IWGIA Yearbook 1989. pp 230-243. Copenhagen.

Gray, A., and K.B. Andersen, 1991 "Report of the Evaluation Trip to Peru for the Project 'Inscription and Titling of Native Communities of the Ucayali'." IWGIA, Copenhagen.

Gray, A., & A. Parellada, 1993. "Inscription, Demarcation and Extension of Indigenous Territories and the Recognition of Communal Reserves in the Central Peruvian Rainforest." IWGIA, Copenhagen.

Gray, A., & K.B. Andersen, 1993."Evaluation Report of the DANIDA/IWGIA Titling and Communal Reserve Project in Ucayali Region, Peru" IWGIA, Copenhagen.

Gray, A, Parellada, A & H. Newing (eds.) 1998. From Principles to Practice: Indigenous Peoples and Biodiversity Conservation in Latin America. IWGIA Document No. 87, Copenhagen.

Hvalkof, S., 1990 "Report Supervision Travel October-November 1990 Landtitling in the Ucayali 5th Evaluation of the Convenio AIDESEP-Ministerio de Agriculture, Peru." IWGIA, Copenhagen.

Hvalkof, S., and A. Gray, 1990a "Supervision Report on Land titling Project, Peruvian Amazon: 'Inscription and Titling of Native Communities in the Ucayali Department'. Report to IWGIA." Copenhagen.

Hvalkof, S., and A. Gray, 1990b "Update Report Land titling in the Peruvian Amazon: the Ucayali Department." IWGIA, Copenhagen.

Instituto Indigenista Peruano, 1989 "Informe Final Sobre las Medidas Referentes a los Derechos, al Bienestar y al Desarrollo de las Etnias nativas de la Zona de Atalaya." Documento elaborado por el Equipo Tecnico nominado por la Comision Multisectorial conformada por la Resolución Ministerial No. 083-88-PCM. Lima.

IWGIA, 1992 "Final Report of Project ,Inscription and Titling of Indigenous Communities in the Ucayali Region, Peruvian Amazon'." Copenhagen.

IWGIA, 1996 "Final Report of Project 'Inscription, Demarcation and Extension of Indigenous Territories and the Recognition of Communal Reserves in the Central Peruvian Rainforest'." Copenhagen.

Parellada, A., 1994. "Report of the DANIDA/IWGIA Titling and Communal Reserves Project in Ucayali Region - Peru." IWGIA, Copenhagen.

Parellada, A & K.B. Andersen, 1995 " Report of the Trip to Peru and Ecuador: The Titling and Communal Reserves Project in Ucayali region - Peru." IWGIA, Copenhagen.

Parellada, A & K.B. Andersen, 1996. "Report of the Trip to Peru and Ecuador: The Titling and Communal Reserves Project in Ucayali region - Peru." IWGIA, Copenghagen.

Parellada, A, 1997. „Report of the Land Titling Project in Ucayali". Copenhagen.
Renard Casevitz, M-F., 1980 „Contrasts between Amerindian and Colonist Land Use in the Southern Peruvian Amazon" in F. Barbira-Scazzocchio, (ed.) Land, People and Planning in Contemporary Amazonia. Cambridge University Centre of Latin American Studies.

PHOTOGRAPHERS

authors	pages
Pablo Lasansky	13, 33, 37, 40, 45, 52, 53, 60, 61, 99 (top), 102 (top), 103 (top), 106, 110, 111 (top), 177, 193, 206 and 207
Alejandro Parellada	36, 41, 56, 57 (bottom), 77, 81, 99 (bottom), 129, 147, 180 (bottom), 181, 185 (bottom), 188, 189 and 211.
Søren Hvalkof	52 (bottom), 102 (bottom), 103 (bottom), 107, 111 (bottom) and 163.
Henrik Lund	31 (top), 44 and 57 (top)
Casiano Aguirre	180 (bottom) and 185 (top)
Other authors	21, 31 (bottom), 44, 67 and 184: AIDESEP 89 (top): by Krohle and Hübner. 89 (bottom): in "War of Shadows"(Brown, Michael and Fernández, Eduardo), 1991: University of California Press: Berkeley. 149: AntiSlavery International